MW00831786

SELF AND NON-SELF

SELF AND NON-SELF

The Drigdriśyaviveka Attributed to Śaṁkara

Translated from the Sanskrit
with a Commentary by

RAPHAEL

Āśram Vidyā Order

Foreword by A.J. Alston

KEGAN PAUL INTERNATIONAL

London and New York

This book was originally published in Italian
as Drgdrśyaviveka by Āśram Vidyā in 1977
Translated from the Italian by Kay McCarthy

First published in English in 1990 by
Kegan Paul International Limited
PO Box 256, London WC1B 3SW, England

Distributed by
John Wiley & Sons Ltd
Southern Cross Trading Estate
1 Oldlands Way, Bognor Regis
West Sussex, PO22 9SA, England

Routledge, Chapman and Hall Inc
29 West 35th Street
New York, NY 10001, USA

The Canterbury Press Pty Ltd
Unit 2, 71 Rushdale Street
Scoresby, Victoria 3179, Australia

© Āśram Vidyā 1990

Set in Baskerville 11/13 point by Columns of Reading

Printed in Great Britain by TJ Press

No part of this book may be reproduced in any form without permission from the publisher, except for the quotation of brief passages in criticism

British Library Cataloguing in Publication Data
Raphael
Self and non-self: the Drigdrisyaviveka attributed to Sankara.
1. Advaita vedanta
I. Title II. Sakaracarya. Drigdrisyaviveka
181′.482

ISBN 0–7103–0377–7

US Library of Congress Cataloging in Publication Data
Applied for

It is necessary to distinguish between Being, and being this or that: between "I am what I am" and "I am this or that", between revealing oneself without name or form, and living for a name and a form; only an act of profound discrimination can allow us to recognize the essential nature of our true Being.

Raphael

CONTENTS

FOREWORD

It is generally agreed today that, with the decline of belief in orthodox Christianity, the West stands in need of spiritual refreshment and instruction, and many are looking to the great mystical teachers of both Christian and non-Christian traditions for the satisfaction of this need. In response to this situation the West has been exposed to a flood of gurus from India, of whom some have been sincere purveyors of sweetness and light, while others have actually revelled in and encouraged those demoniac tendencies which have brought so much misery to our industrialized society. In the absence of a reliable consumer's guide, the western seeker needs to test what he is being offered in the light of those spiritual traditions in India which are rooted in the wisdom of the ancient sages and have stood the test of time. Kegan Paul International are to be congratulated for undertaking the publication of both technical and (relatively) popular works in this field.

SELF AND NON-SELF, here published with full English commentary and transliterated Sanskrit text, is a popular exposition of Shankara's Advaita Vedanta, and is accepted in India as a sound introduction to the basic principles of the system. The full commentary will help acquaint the beginner with the inevitable technical terms, and the transliterated Sanskrit text will be of use in various ways to students at different stages. The parallels drawn in the commentary with Plotinus, St. Augustine and other western figures add to the value of the work, and scholars will welcome the truly monumental bibliography based mainly on the work of Professor Mario Piantelli. All in all, a helpful book for the spiritual enquirer and a standard exposition of classical Advaita Vedanta for the student of comparative religion.

A.J. Alston
London, 1989

INTRODUCTION

If we take a piece of clay and make a jar from it and this jar one day becomes aware of itself, it will say: I am a jar.

If we break down the jar and re-knead the clay and make a statue and one day the statue becomes conscious of itself, it will say: I am a statue.

If we break down the statue and re-knead what gave origin to the jar and to the statue and make a pyramid of it and this becomes aware of itself it will say: I am a pyramid.

But if the jar, the statue and the pyramid – spatial-temporal constructions qualified by certain forms – could really become aware of their *primordial* and *existential* unconscious substratum they would say: I am formless, homogeneous clay that takes form now as a jar, now as a statue, now as a pyramid.

Beyond every formal-structural 'modification', beyond all ego-form-quality the substratum that is pure Existence (*sat*) lives eternally.

Sat is that undivided essence always identical to itself which gives life-appearance to all that exists or, better still, to all that is perceived. There is no 'empircal ego', whatever condition it may belong to, which does not feel within itself, in an innate way, this eternally pulsing *presence*. Descartes states: 'I can doubt everything, except the fact that I think, therefore I really exist'. This existence does not need either demonstration or philosophical or scientific arguments. The very existence of the ego-man (as an entity separated from the context of life) is the reflection of *Sat*: Life that is not born and does not die. *Sat* is *Brahman*, the substratum of all, in that it is real Existence without change or alteration; Absolute Life, pure Being from which motion-change-cause comes.

'What does not exist can not be brought into existence; what exists can not cease to exist. This ultimate truth was revealed by those who saw the essence of things'.

'Know that *That*, from which all this [manifested, changing] emanates, is indestructible. No one can cause the destruction of the unperishable Being'.

'It was never born, nor does it ever die. Having always been, it can not cease to be. Non-born, permanent, imperishable, ancient, it is not killed even when the body is killed'.[1]

Śaṁkara asks himself: What is Being? What is non-being? In his commentary to the above-mentioned *sūtras* he states that non-being (*abhāva*) is that which does not really exist, has no sufficient reason and has no intrinsic life of its own. This definition includes all the expressions of existence upon the perceptible plane. If we analyse every experience, we note a chain of effects which, in turn, are simple *modifications* or alterations; from this we can deduce that the objective-empirical world has only a changeable and phenomenal value.

The universe is only an 'uninterrupted flow of image-forms'. But a modification is just a more or less different aspect from its cause; basically it is the cause that presents itself in a new event-framework. Now, we can not take in both cause and effect at a single glance: we can see the one or the other. Empirical experience is based upon this concep-

[1] *Bhagavad-Gītā*: 16–17–20. Translated and commented upon by Raphael, Edizioni Āśram Vidyā, Roma.

tion of cause and effect; the perceptible shows itself as a hierarchy of these two terms, but what is now effect later may appear as cause, and a cause may prove to be an effect. Fundamentally these two terms can be equalled, they belong to the same denominator; they are simply categories that change constantly and therefore they can not have any absolute Reality. Beyond cause-effect-cause etc., there is *Sat*: absolute Life-Existence without cause and without effect; we might say uncaused.

According to *Vedānta*, the universal basis of Being is the *ātman* or *Brahman-nirguṇa*. Non-being or becoming is a *māyā*-phenomenon, which is not 'illusion' in the Western sense of the word, but a word which etymologically means 'that which flows, changes every moment, which appears and disappears'.

For *Advaita Vedānta* the universe of names and forms (cause-effect-cause etc.) is a production of *māyā*. As long as we remain within the realm of causes and effects, we are prisoners of *māyā*, that is of the principle of causality. There is only one means by which to eliminate the veil of *māyā*: that of considering cause-effect as a simple *superimposition* upon *Brahman*. When all the superimpositions disappear, then Reality will reveal itself as *Sat*, Existence without change and without any transformation, therefore without conflict. Where there is becoming there is time-space, where there is time-space there is imprisonment and limitation, where there are these there is conflict and bewilderment.

The mayahic manifestation can be seen under two different lights:

– from the absolute *Brahman* point of view it has no degree of reality.
– from the empirical point of view we can consider it, as stated by the *Māṇḍūkya Upaniṣad*, as a homogeneous unity divided into three parts; the fourth part remains the transcendent and the uncaused:

I *The gross state*: the totality of living beings having a name and a form; it is the totality of physical bodies.

II *The subtle state*: is the cosmic mental state, the psychic life of universal existence. The gross state emerges from the subtle one. Man's mind itself is an infinitesimal fraction of this cosmic Mind. There is no manifested form, at any level or in any state whatever, that does not possess a portion of the cosmic Mind. It corresponds to *taijasa* (the shining).

III *The causal state*: this contains within itself virtually all the infinite expressions of universal Life. Here everything is at the potential state. It corresponds to *prājña*.

These three states are also compared to the conditions of waking, dreaming and deep sleep where awareness retires into the potential state.

The Fourth can be described only through negation: Non-Born, Non-Being, in that it is pure Being, Non-Manifest, Unconditioned, Uncaused, Infinite, Absolute. It is not the 'known', nor is it what the mind imagines as the unknown, it is not a 'state' either. It corresponds to *Turīya* and can be reached by *nirvikalpa-samādhi*. From the Absolute point of view, as we have already said, manifestation has no reality.

The above-mentioned *Upaniṣad* says:

'The first quarter (*pāda*) is *vaiśvānara*, whose sphere (of action) is waking; it is conscious of external objects, has seven limbs and nineteen mouths; it experiences gross (material) objects'.

'The second quarter (*pāda*) is *taijasa* (the luminous) whose sphere of action is the state of dreaming; the consciousness has withdrawn within itself. It has seven limbs and nineteen mouths and experiences subtle objects'.

'This is the state of deep sleep where the sleeper does not enjoy any object or dream any dream. The third quarter (*pāda*) is *prājña*, whose sphere of action is, in fact, deep sleep; in it all things remain undifferentiated; in truth it is a unity of pure awareness. (In *prājña*) there is complete happiness and the sleeper actually enjoys this happiness. It is the cognitive condition (of the other two states)'.

'The Wise think that the Fourth, which has no knowledge either of the internal (subjective) world nor of the external (objective) world nor of both at the same time, and which, finally, is not (even) a unity of integral consciousness, as it is neither awareness nor unawareness, is *adṛṣṭa*: invisible, *avyavahārya*: non-acting, *agrāhya*: incomprehensible, *alakṣaṇa*: undefinable, *acintya*: unthinkable, *avyapadeśya*: indescribable; it is the only *pratyayasāra*: the essence of self-knowledge, without trace of manifestation, full of peace and bliss without duality: it is *ātman* and as such must be known'.[1]

'With three-quarters of Myself I manifest myself' states the Sacred Indian Scripture, 'but if all these things procede from Me, I am not these things'; they are simple shadows-lights projected upon the screen of the Infinite. Beyond all chemical compounds, nitrogen, water, hydrogen, iron etc. – shadows thrown upon a fragment of time-space – there exists only undifferentiated electrical substance always equal to itself. Thus, if a plane is composed of lines these are composed of points and the point, although without dimension, is the basic aspect of all manifested forms. *Sat* is Reality, the ultimate Reality; it is pure, uncontaminated Life, in the unqualified, a-formal state.

---

[1] *Māṇḍūkya Upaniṣad with the kārikā-verses of Gauḍapāda and commentary by Śaṁkara*: I, III, IV, V, VII: translated into Italian from Sanskrit by Raphael, notes by Raphael, Edizioni Āśram Vidyā, Roma 1976.

Śaṁkara invites us to discriminate (*viveka*) between Real and unreal, between Self and non-Self, between Infinite and finite, between Life and death. Man's greatest conflicts stem from his attachment to and his identification with the non-Self, with the finite, with the unreal, in other words with death. Knowledge leads to the recognition of *a-Sat* (false existence) and the discovery of *Sat* (True Existence).

Sat includes *cit*, absolute Intelligence. As *Sat* is not a simple quality, but the very essence of all that is, thus *cit*, besides being a quality, is a consubstantiality of *sat*.

Edison says: 'It seems to me that every atom has a certain quantity of primigenial intelligence . . .'.

This intelligence, with existence, constitutes the sole basis of every life-form; it is the support of all relative knowledge and it is by it that we can acquire awareness of the objective world, of the subjective world and of the *Ens in se*. If this intelligible light were to fail, perception itself would cease to function. This light, which reveals everything, is not revealed because it can not be considered an object of knowledge. The Absolute can never be considered an object of perception because this would imply duality. The Absolute simply *is*. *Light-Awareness-Intelligence* is, we can say, an *a priori* principle of our very existence (as a phenomenal aspect) because the mind does not produce it but it is revealed through what men call mind. How can thought-mind, which is cause-time-space, grasp what is without cause or time or space?

We should remember that the human mind is not the only medium of 'The Light that reveals all'; every atom of the Universe, we have seen, reveals *principial* Intelligence at different levels.

It is above all through *cit* that the *Vedānta* pursues Brahmanic Realization. *Advaita* is *practical* metaphysics which must be experimented in the world of becoming. This metaphysical pathway, by availing of the reflection of *cit*, as *viveka* (discernment, intellective super-conscious intuition), realizes brahmanic Identity in a concrete way. The life-substratum, which never undergoes change, is *sat*; the mode through which *sat* manifests itself is *cit*; the intrinsic vibration that permeates *sat* and *cit* is *ānanda*, absolute Fulfilment-Bliss.

In the *Taittirīya Upaniṣad* (III, VI, 1) we read:

> 'In truth these living creatures were born of Bliss, it is through Bliss that, having come into existence, they are kept alive, it is to Bliss that they will all return'.

The irresistible motion that gives rise to, sustains and, in time and space, causes all forms of manifested life to transcend is made up of *ānanda*. This can not be revealed totally until differentiation is transcended.

The reflections of *ānanda* in the incarnated *jīva* are those sensorial pleasures that go from sex to the refined pleasure of intellectual, spiritual and aesthetic things. There is no manifest atom that does not move and tend towards the state of happiness. By an act of love man is born to life, by an act of love he sacrifices himself, by an act of love the sun and the other stars move. The individual acts, urged by the universal force of 'pleasure'. Passions are an altered form of this innate beatific nature. Passion is enjoyment, sentiment is gratification of pleasure; even intellectual research is the fruit of pleasure, of satisfaction. However, sensory enjoyment, of any dimension whatever, is not *ānanda*, but a simple distorted reflection. Thus intelligence-instinct, whether mineral, vegetable, animal or human, is not brahmanic *cit*, just as the weak lunar gleam is not the blinding light of the sun. The entire world of names and forms emerges from the urge of *ānanda*, is preserved by *ānanda*, is transformed and destroyed by a pure act of Fulfilment. Realization itself, is born of *ānanda*. For love of the beloved, the mystic-*bhakta* transcends the relative; for love of truth, *jñāni* finds *sat* within himself – Brahmanic Existence without parts; for love of the one Life, the incarnated *jīva* abandons the forms by dying to itself. Death, therefore, is the effect of an act of love towards great homogeneous Life. Death is Liberation.

Only through *samādhi* the individual can really understand the power of the highest bliss that can be reached within the manifested sphere. His sheath-vehicle (*ānanda-maya-kośa*), the last, starting from below, is full and permeated by this essence of brahmanic Joy.

He has within himself the inexhaustible source of *sattvic* (pure) happiness, but he does not make use of it; he has within himself the highest expression of beatitude, but, identifying with other sheaths, he prefers dualist emotional appetites with their consequent opposite states. He lives in pleasure-pain because he wants to. Strange paradox: life, born by an act of love, is often mortified by the darkest pain, by the blindest despair and by the most bitter resentment.

The *Taittirīya Upaniṣad* (II, v, 1) states:

> 'The *ānanda-maya-kośa* [sheath of Bliss] has the exact proportions of the human body; it is identical to the gross physical body, even if much more subtle: tenderness is the head, happiness is the right shoulder, pleasure the left shoulder, Bliss is the Self and *Brahman* itself is the base, the support'.

The more we tend towards egoistic and material enjoyment the more *ānanda* is obscured and remains latent; the more we reach up to attain the super-individual condition, sublimating sensory desire, the source of all conflict, the more strongly *ānanda* emerges. We can say that *sat* and *cit* are expressed more than *ānanda*. According to the classical *Vedānta*, reality has five characteristics: *sat*, *cit*, *ānanda*, *nāma* (name) and *rūpa* (form). We perceive names and forms by means of the *vṛttis* of the internal organ or *antaḥkaraṇa*. Of the presence of *sat* and *cit* we have intuitive certainty while *ānanda* is accessible only to those whose minds are permeated by pure *sattva*. Therefore, happiness can not manifest itself except in pure thinking and can be obscured more easily than *sat* and *cit*, thus we can discover it only after severe ascesis (*sādhanā*). Realization, which is the ultimate aim of manifested life, is achieved by eliminating in oneself all traces of *rajas* and *tamas* (extroverted desire and material inertia). When the mental state, free from *rajas* and *tamas*, is raised up to its *sattvic* vibratory state, it produces only thought in harmony with the *ānanda* sheath. Reality thus presents itself in a far more extensive light; this state of being identifies with supreme Happiness. Let us remember that *sat*, *cit* and *ānanda* belong to the sphere of the absolute *Brahman* and therefore can not be considered as qualifications, attributes, conditions or causes except from the empirical point of view.

Ānanda represents an innate, natural modality of pure Bliss and absolute Fullness of *Brahman*. Pleasure-pain, good-evil, anxiety and anguish are qualities belonging to becoming, to the ego-jar (ego-man), ego-statue etc. Cause-effect-cause etc., mean birth-death-birth, endless and conflictual. Where can we find *pax profunda*? Where the placid serenity of the pacified heart? It is not to be found in the ebb and flow of the world of names and forms, certainly not in the continual modification of consciousness, nor in continuous research, nor in gratifying the egoistic phantom, but simply in the Substratum that is always identical to itself and which is *Brahman-ānanda*. Pacified are those who have recovered their formless 'original' condition; they unveil *ānanda*: absolute Bliss and serenity. To say absolute *Sat*-Existence means to say *Ānanda*-Bliss. These terms are not separate, they are two expressions of a sole essence. On the other hand, Absolute Existence can not but contain within itself this Bliss-Fullness. Sensory happiness is the qualification of a state of momentary adhesion, participation, approval and so on. But *ānanda* is not a state of mind or of consciousness, just as Life is not a state of mind or of perception. Life *is*. *Ānanda is*. We can only grasp a mere reflection of such a possibility if we think of a being devoid of all desire because totally gratified. This being, we can say, is pacified; no desire-thought-wave disturbs him, he remains in the full and beatified condition of being. Wanting nothing, possessing all. In the *Pañcadaśī* we read:

> 'The nature of the indivisible being is represented by supreme Bliss'.

If sensory happiness is the outcome of objectual (gross or subtle) satisfaction, *ānanda* is the Bliss that is born of its own existence, of its intrinsic nature. In the former case there is duality, in the second unity and completeness.

> 'I am *sat-cit-ānanda*, independent, self-resplendent, free from duality . . .'.
>
> (*Dṛgdṛśyaviveka*: 25)

Śaṁkara dedicated the following poem to *Brahman* as *cit* and *ānanda*:

> 1. I am neither mind, nor intellect, nor thought, nor ego-sense [*manas*, *buddhi*, *citta*, *ahaṁkāra*, the four aspects of the internal organ or *antaḥkaraṇa*];
> I am neither sight, nor taste, nor smell, nor hearing;
> I am neither ether, nor earth, nor air, nor fire;
> I am absolute pure Intelligence (*cit*) and Bliss (*ānanda*);
> I am *Śiva*, I am *Śiva*! [The formula by which identity of *jīva* with *Brahman*, here personified by *Śiva*, is proclaimed].
>
> 2. I am neither energy nor the five vital breaths;
> I am neither the seven elements of the material body [the seven *dhātus*: flesh, skin, bones, marrow, blood, fat, seminal liquid], nor the five sheaths that compose the individualized soul [*annamaya-kośa*, *prāṇamaya-kośa*, *manomaya-kośa*, *vijñānamaya-kośa*, *ānandamaya-kośa*];

I am not the five organs of action;
I am pure Intelligence (*cit*) and Bliss (*ānanda*);
I am *Śiva*, I am *Śiva*!

3. I feel neither attraction nor repulsion, nor greed nor deceit;
I feel neither envy nor pride;
I have no duty to carry out nor aim to pursue;
I am pure Intelligence and Bliss;
I am *Śiva*, I am *Śiva*!

4. I am neither good, nor evil, nor pleasure, nor suffering;
I am not the sacred word [*mantra*], nor the pilgrimage, nor the Scriptures, nor the sacrificial act;
I am not he who eats, nor what is eaten, nor am I the act of eating;
I am pure Intelligence and Bliss;
I am *Śiva*, I am *Śiva*!

5. I know not death, nor fear, nor caste distinction;
I have neither father, nor mother, nor birth, nor friends, nor relatives, nor master, nor disciples [as absolute *Brahman* one is beyond every condition connected with manifested *jīva* and therefore all its attributes];
I am pure Intelligence and Bliss;
I am *Śiva*, I am *Śiva*!

6. I am without modification, without form, I am Infinite, All-pervading;
Nothing can corrode my nature: neither sensory attachment nor liberation, nor the object of knowledge;
I am pure Intelligence and Bliss;
I am *Śiva*, I am *Śiva*!

The *Dṛgdṛśyaviveka* (*Dṛg* = Spectator-observer, *dṛśya* = spectacle, *viveka* = discrimination) is a rational discriminating method for distinguishing between the Spectator and the spectacle (Self and non-Self). It is of extreme importance for a deep understanding of *Vedānta* and is considered a classic. The forty-six *sūtras* in this text demonstrate rationally that the Observer is distinct from the observed (the world of names and forms) and that *jīva* (living individuality) not being an Absolute must merge into *Brahman*.

At the beginning, the eye that sees seems to be the observer, then thought, which is itself the object of perception, becomes the observer, until we arrive at an observer that can not be the object of sensory knowledge. The Witness (*ātman*) observes the performance of the film-spectacle (as the spectator sees the sequence of images at the cinema), understands the movement that takes place in the mind and persists even after the show is over or has been interrupted.

All new experiences are projected necessarily upon the indestructible atmic or brahmanic substratum. Every experiment gives rise, at the same time, to a subject and an object, an observer and a spectacle, indissolubly associated with one another. *Ātman-Brahman* is the substratum common to the two elements of experience. These postulates are the peculiar characteristics and the aims of the *Advaita* (One-without-a-second).

In the *Dṛgdṛśyaviveka*, besides, the following are given: a detailed description of the different kinds of concentration (*samādhi*), the three theories concerning *jīva* empirically and that regarding the *upādhis*-sheaths of the *jīva* itself, and other questions of primary importance to *Vedānta* teaching.

Svāmi Nikhilānanda writes: 'This work, which contains only forty-six *ślokas* is an excellent vademecum for students of advanced courses in *Advaita* philosophy'.

Verses 13 to 31 (excluding 14, 21, and 28) are to be found in a minor *Upaniṣad* entitled *Sarasvatīrahasya upaniṣad*.

The author's identity is uncertain: some attribute the authorship of the *Dṛgdṛśyaviveka* to Bhāratī-tīrtha. The commentator Ānandajñāna, on the basis of certain manuscripts, attributes it to Śaṁkara.

Niścala-dāsa attributes it to Vidyāraṇya who also wrote the vedantic philosophical treatise *Pañcadaśī*.

Bhāratī-tīrtha, *guru* of Vidyāraṇya, was the grand Master

of the Monastery of Śṛṅgeri, founded by Śaṁkara. Whoever the author may be, the text reflects the traditional vedantic conception, especially that of Śaṁkara, and the authorship has little importance.

The square brackets found in the text have been added by us.

R.

THE DRIGDRIŚYAVIVEKA

1. An object-form is perceived, but it is the eye which perceives. This is perceived by the mind which becomes the perceiving subject. Then, the mind, with its modifications, is perceived by the Thinker-Spectator who cannot be the object of perception.

All forms are simply agglomerations of energy, which manifest certain peculiar qualities, living in time and space. A mineral, a vegetable, an animal, a human body, a planet, a star, etc., are but the result of vibrations. What does seeing an object entail? It means that our eyes respond to the vibrations of light coming from the object, then, our mind transforms them into concepts of form and name; in other words, the mind crystallizes the flow of life. No form is as stable or compact as we might imagine; it is a rhythmical flux, a vibrating wave of light in perpetual movement. All perception is based upon ondulatory vibrations. If we understand all this, the old tri-dimensional world will appear to us as a play of rhythm-waves upon the screen of the Infinite. The compound universe breaks down into vibrating phenomena: mine, yours, his, hers dissolve and the individual consciousness experiences the simple, indifferentiated, universal sound of Being. The manifested world, both gross and subtle, is the spectacle, he who witnesses the spectacle is the observer.

Between the observed and the observer there must be a link-instrument, a binding factor, otherwise they would be completely disjointed from one another with no possibility of 'knowing each other'. This instrument is the individual consciousness. This – mechanism of contact which causes awareness – is the connection which unites the observer and the spectacle. Thus three data come to the discriminating attention of whoever wants to begin deepening his knowledge of *realizative* philosophy: observer (subject), individual consciousness, object. The West – in general – has taken an interest in and is interested in the object; the tendency is objectivistic. The East is more subjectivistic and is interested above all in the subject. *Advaita Vedānta*, the metaphysics of the 'One-without-a-second', does not follow either of these two tendencies because it states that beyond both object and subject there is *Brahman nirguṇa*, the Unconditioned, the ever Existing, the Uncaused, the Substratum of the whole spectacle and of the individualized perceiver-spectator. The spectacle is first perceived by the eye – of course the eye here represents all the five senses – the eye itself is also the object of perception; and finally the mind, as thought, presupposes a thinker – thus thought too becomes the object of perception and a part of the spectacle. Can we perceive him who perceives? For *Vedānta* it is not possible to perceive the subject because by being perceived he would not be a knowing subject but a simple *object* of knowledge. 'We can not dance on top of our own shoulders', says the old Hindu proverb. We can sensorially see, hear, touch everything except for the one revealed through these aspects. At this level the Spectator lives in Silence. As long as there is a spectacle-object, there is space-time and duality; when the spectacle is no longer there, Unity emerges rotating upon its own axis; when the Unity merges into the Unconditioned, it discovers itself to be *Brahman*-without-a-second.

The modifications of the mind to which the *śloka* refers are:

- *buddhi*: the discriminating mind-intellect; when purified it works through intuitive discernment;
- *ahaṁkāra*: the sense of ego and of distinction;
- *manas*: sensory perception, perceiving mind, psychic faculties.

The observer is the incarnated *jīva* which is the reflection of *ātman* itself. It is this *jīva* which, all told, perceives; when its attention is elsewhere, the eyes, while seeing, do not really see, the ears, while hearing, do not really hear, and the vocal organ, while speaking, does not truly speak.

Let us clarify some terms that are repeated in the text:

- Spectator-Witness: unconditioned *ātman*.
- Experimenter: *jīva*, the embodied soul.
- Spectacle: any object of knowledge including ideas, emotions, etc.

In the text these terms will be adequately treated.

2. Due to distinctions such as: blue, yellow, gross or subtle, short or long, etc., the eye, as a unity, perceives the variety of forms.

In the field of music, when we admit the existence of the various notes, we create a distinction, a multiplicity of data, but it is obvious that these notes presuppose the existence of a common homogeneous sole and undivided substratum which is sound. Sound *is*, while the notes *appear* to our perception as separate and absolute entities. We say 'appear' because, in truth, they never cease to be sound. The world of names and forms which compose the spectacle (*dṛśya*) is perceived as something *distinct* from the substratum out of which it arose. A form-object, we have already said, is the product of a particular vibratory state in continual transformation, which has no life of its own distinct from all other vibratory states.

3. The eye [sight] is penetrating, clouded or else it is blind: and these characteristics can be perceived because the mind is a unity. This applies, too, to [all the other organs]: ear, skin, etc.

When the eye undergoes a change, this is perceived by the mind, because the mind synthesizes all the senses.

The perceptive sequence is as follows:

- object;
- organ of contact or sensory mind;
- the intellect which transposes the object into the field of concepts;
- experimenter.

Each factor is perceived by the successive ones; perception could not exist, if at any stage of the chain a link were missing.

According to *Vedānta* metaphysics, perception occurs because the experimenting subject projects his mental faculty onto the object. It is not the object which enters the mind and moulds it, but it is the subject's mind, like an elephant's trunk, which directs itself towards the object, takes in its form or model, creating sensation. Hence all the *yoga* techniques for dominating the perceiving mind.

4. Consciousness illuminates desire, decisiveness and uncertainty, faith and incredulity, perseverance and inconstancy, humility, understanding, fear, etc., because [It] is a unity.

Consciousness is here identified with everlasting *cit*. It is light – undifferentiated in itself – which illuminates all the indefinite mental modifications. When the object disappears Consciousness reflects Itself as *cit* in the non-manifested state.

5. This [Consciousness] has neither birth nor growth nor death; It is always self-resplendent, depending upon nothing else, It illuminates all things.

'In it [*ātman*] neither sun nor moon nor stars shine, lightning does not flash nor this fire of ours; all this universe shines with its light'.

(*Kaṭha up.*: II, V, 15)

The absolute Consciousness (*cit*) can not be born nor can it die, it can not have growth or old age; these qualities are however inherent to individualized, empirical, experimenting *jīva*.

'In the golden and glorious sheath dwells the pure and undivided *Brahman*; It is the shining, light of lights, It is that One whom the knowers of the *ātman* know'.

(*Muṇḍaka up.*: II, II, 10)

6. A reflection of pure Consciousness permeates buddhi giving it intelligence. The buddhi reveals itself in its double nature: as selfness and as mind.

Here the difference between pure atmic Consciousness and the relative and phenomenal sheaths which manifest quality and appearance is emphasized. First we have the *ātman* as pure Consciousness. The *ātman* is non-born, non-manifest, without cause, the absolute Witness of the endless series of existential modifications. It is not the *ātman* which acts directly, it is its outer shadows which, animated and stimulated by it, produce determined effects. This condition of being is analogous to that of the atom. We can synthesize here what we have already said in our notes to Śaṁkara's *Vivekacūḍāmaṇi*.[1]

The chemical properties of an atom are exclusively the outcome of the number of electrons that make up the shell-

---

[1] *Vivekacūḍāmaṇi* by Śaṁkara, translated into Italian and commented by Raphael, Edizioni Āśram Vidyā.

sheath of the atom itself. The atomic nucleus remains unaltered, producing all its electronic attributes only indirectly. The *ātman*-nucleus, while remaining deep within the atom-man, produces the properties and qualities of the *upādhi*-sheaths or vehicles of the individualized *jīva* only indirectly, let us say by its very presence. It is beyond all electronic-upadhic change; it is that portion of reflected vehicular consciousness that manifests action, attraction, repulsion, joy, pain, accumulation, birth, development, decline and death. In other words, atmic power – which is the pure light of Existence, Consciousness, Intelligence, Bliss – produces reflections, phenomenon-shades which, permeated by a weak vitality, consciousness and happiness think that they are absolute existences, separated from the first Cause and the primeval generator. We can say: they believe to be absolute causes while they are really only simple effects. Erroneous awareness of the intrinsic and true upadhic state leads the *jīva* – the unity of consciousness which holds the various sheaths together – to consider itself immortal while it is merely a phenomenon which is born, grows and dies.

We mistake the rope for a snake and, as long as the illusion lasts, we really believe that the *jīva* with its body-sheaths is Reality rather than the eternally non-acting *ātman*, the motionless Witness.

The *ātman*, on account of its intrinsic power, gives birth to an energetic nucleus called *buddhi* which, in turn, represents the *jīva*, which produces the body-sheaths of manifestation. But human *jīva* is only a shadow, a mirage, a phenomenon which, constantly in motion and changing, wanders, now attracted by pleasure, now pushed by pain until it reaches its inevitable samsaric end. We can use an analogy: the proper amount of solar fire produces humidity and heat, so that, a cloud, caused by the sun, believes itself to be a vital, absolute, autonomous, separate entity having no connection with the sun. Naturally it is the victim of illusion because –

in reality – it is but a simple phenomenon which has barely time to take form before disappearing again. This misconceived vision is the effect of *māyā*-ignorance or 'magic' which makes the impossible possible or which knows how to hide the true essence of things. But *māyā* itself is not absolute; in fact, the *jīva*, when it reaches maturity becomes aware of its real condition and, no longer nourishing 'illusion', allows itself to be absorbed by true, authentic, absolute Truth-Reality: the *ātman*, the Uncaused, the eternal Witness of the indefinite phenomenal modifications of the *jīva* and its body-sheaths of manifestation.

The projective mental power of the sleeper imagines an entire nocturnal universe which, 'animated' by this power, takes on objectiveness and concreteness. This living world is only the projection of a dream which, although true in time and space, in reality it is only a phenomenal production. This is why Kṛṣṇa – the incarnation of *ātman* – in the *Bhagavad-Gītā* states:

> 'Although this whole universe is produced by me, I am not this universe'.

As we have seen, *buddhi*, as manifested, phenomenal *jīva*, produces the internal organ or *antaḥkaraṇa* composed of the mental and vital sheaths.

7. The Sage considers the reflection [of consciousness] and the sense of ego to be identical just as fire and hot iron are. The body, identifying with its ego, becomes aware of itself.

Here ego is associated with the notion of subject. Thus we have the subject (ego-*jīva*) and the object; beyond subject-object exists the eternal *ātman* without birth and without death.

With regard to identification with non-Self this is what Plotinus says:

'. . . Come, let him who dares enter and follow Its footsteps into the depths; not without having first left outside the vision of his mortal eyes and taking care not to look back at those bodies which were once splendid . . . Even if he once desired them, let him no longer pursue these lovely bodies, and let him know, rather, that they are but images, traces, shadows . . . Let him take refuge in It, the model of those images. Whosoever pounces on these, as if to touch real things, is like him who trying to embrace his image upon the waves – this is, I believe, what the fable [of Narcissus] means – fell into the deep current, and disappeared. Similarly, whosoever is a prisoner of beautiful bodies and does not free himself, falls not with the body but with the soul into the abyss dark and sad for the spirit where, blind, he shall remain, in Hades, and down there too, as here, remain in the company of shadows . . .'.

(Plotinus, *Enneads*: I, 6, VIII)

8. The sense of ego can identify in three ways: with the reflection of consciousness, with the body and with the Witness. The first [identification] is natural, the second is due to previous karma, the third to ignorance.

Once the reflection of consciousness and ego (*ahaṁkāra*) emerge, they identify with one another.

Thus we have Descartes' statement. 'I think, therefore I am'. The result of the two poles, consciousness and separate ego-centre, is the statement: I am perceptive as a separate individual.

The subsequent identification with the body is due to past *karma*; that is, given a specific body-sheath, the memory of this corporeal identification causes us to say: we are so-and-so with a name and form.

Identification with the internal absolute Witness is due to *māyā*, to ignorance. The *jīva*-experimenter takes possession of the *ātman*'s absoluteness thus believing itself to be absolute but it falls into an error of judgement. Here effect is taken to be cause, phenomenon for noumenon.

> 'One looks into Oneself as into a mirror, like in a dream, in the world of Manes, like in waters in the world of Gandharvas, like light and heat in the world of *Brahman*'.
>
> 'The *manas* transcends perceptible objects, the *buddhi* transcends the *manas* [individualized mind], the great *ātman* transcends the *buddhi* and the Non-Manifest transcends all'.
>
> (*Kaṭha Up.*: II, VI, 5–7)

It is necessary to ponder upon the fact that the *jīva* (simple phenomenal fraction) can not believe itself to be *ātman*, remaining in its condition of separate *jīva*. The part can not be the Whole, nor can the phenomenon represent the noumenon.

9. The reciprocal and natural identification [of the ego and the reflection of consciousness] lasts as long as it is considered real; the other two identifications will vanish when the effects of the karma pass and Illumination emerges.

Every time an idea emerges we note that the subject, the object and the link between them appear simultaneously. The mental part is as the hub of a wheel, all the spokes are linked to it and they transmit different impulses; this is how the wheel of rebirth (*saṁsāra*) turns, and the ego creates the notion of time, space and causality. As long as the *jīva* and its mental modifications are held to be true it is obvious that *māyā* remains equally substantial and sure. Śaṁkara holds that the world of names and forms is real for whoever identifies with *māyā*, just as a dream is real to the dreamer, therefore he neither denies the empirical world nor opposes it. Identification with the body disappears when all the effects of *karma* cease; the end of *karma* can occur when the generating cause has exhausted itself or when one achieves Realization (*mokṣa*). During deep sleep and the interval between two samsaric rebirths, *karma* is only suspended and remains in the latent state.

When the *jīva* believes itself to be absolute, distinct from the *ātman-Brahman* and defines itself as self existent, then only supreme Knowledge, ultimate Knowledge, can free this phantom from the error into which it has fallen. Ignorance can be removed and resolved by knowledge, but in this case it is not intellectual, erudite knowledge we are speaking of. We must ponder upon these important equalities:

Knowledge = Realization
Realization = Liberation

Liberation is the effect of the "immersion" or rather of the disappearance of the *jīva* into the *ātman-Brahman*; just like the disappearance of an atomic compound occurs when mass becomes formless energy.

10. In deep sleep [prājña] when the ego disappears, the body itself loses awareness. In dreams [taijasa] there is only the semi-emergence of the ego, while in waking [vaiśvānara] the ego is fully aware.

These three states, considered here psychologically, are treated by Gauḍapāda from a doctrinal and metaphysical point of view in the *kārikā*-verses of the *Māṇḍūdya Upaniṣad*. Furthermore, in these verses the 'Fourth' and ultimate state, that of *Turīya*, is described (see the extract from the *Upaniṣad* quoted in the Introduction at page 7).

Brahman is seen from the point of view of the individual condition as having four aspects, therefore we can speak of multiple states of Being. Three are in time and space, one is beyond them. When the Liberated achieves *nirvikalpa samādhi* he transcends the causal, gross and subtle manifest world, and merges into the One-without-a-second. Manifestation is exteriorized in the space-time-causality framework and has its archetypical potentiality in the Unmanifested. In the gross condition, the totality of physical, planetary and cosmic bodies form the whole of the solid material state. But there are two other cosmic or universal states: the subtle and the causal which are usually beyond our comprehension. We must keep in mind that *Īśvara*, *Hiranyagarbha*, etc. . . . are not 'individuals', are not anthropomorphic aspects, they are 'principles'. Since *Īśvara* is considered the God-person, we must remember that *person*, in the traditional sense, means 'principle'.

Here is a synthetic picture which should make everything clear:

Turīya – The Fourth – Brahman

		Macrocosm	Microcosm
Manifestation	Causal	*Īśvara*	*Prājña*
	Subtle	*Hiranyagarbha*	*Taijasa*
	Gross	*Virāṭ*	*Vaiśvānara*

For the Awakened, the subtle and gross states (dream and waking) have exactly the same value: they represent a simple idea. The world is only a 'thought' of God at various vibratory levels.

11. The internal organ, which is a modification, identifying with the reflection of Consciousness imagines ideas while dreaming. While in the waking state and in relation with the sensory organs, it imagines external objects.

The internal organ (*antaḥkaraṇa*) includes: *manas*, *citta*, *buddhi*, *ahaṁkāra*. Let us define these terms better: *citta* is mental substance, a part of the great cosmic Mind (*Mahat*); it is the general name given to the mind and to all its numberless modifications; it represents the total contents of the mind. When *citta* is spurred by an internal or external stimulus – transmitted by the senses (*indriya*) – it vibrates producing a wave (*vṛtti*) just like a magnetic tape when stimulated by electrical impulses bearing messages; the wave is analysed by empirical perception or *manas*, and *buddhi* determines its understanding and deliberation. In this final phase the conceptual formulation and the distinction between things occurs. *Ahaṁkāra* is the sense of ego and of distinction. The entire process examined constitutes the *antaḥkaraṇa*, the internal perceptive organ, the mental process of reception, analysis and transmission.

Antaḥkaraṇa, which is itself produced by movement, imagines subtle objects when dreaming and gross objects when waking. Now, as already seen, for *Vedānta* these two states do not differ because both can be reduced to mental images. If a datum can not exist without perception, we must say that an object is perception-sensation; thus the whole field of existence is sensation-perception.

'. . . but, as It is beyond being, It is also beyond thought'.
(*Enneads*: V, 6, VI)

12. The insensible subtle body, the material cause of the manas and of the sense of ego, is a unity; it passes progressively through the three states [waking, dreaming and deep sleep] and it is subject to birth and death.

The subtle body (*liṅga* or *sūkṣma-śarīra*) represents *antaḥkaraṇa* or the internal organ. According to some Vedantic texts it is composed of seventeen elements:

Jñāna-indriya (organs of perception)	*śrotra* (hearing) *tvac* (touch) *cakṣus* (sight) *rasana* (taste) *ghrāṇa* (smell)
Karma-indriya (organs of action)	*pāyu* (excretion) *upastha* (generation) *pāni* (hands) *pāda* (feet) *vāc* (voice)
Prāṇa (vital breaths)	*prāṇa* (appropriation) *apāna* (elimination) *vyāna* (distribution) *udāna* (expression) *samāna* (assimilation)
Manas	sensorial or egoical mind
Buddhi	pure reason or intuitive discernment

Antaḥkaraṇa is a modification of *avidyā*-ignorance and seems to be animated because it is associated with the reflection of *cit*; it undergoes the conditioning of birth, growth, old age, decline and death.

All the activity belonging to the first two kinds of organs, of perception (*jñāna-indriya*) and of action (*karma-indriya*), is voluntary, while that belonging to the pranic organ and its five-fold modification is involuntary. A *yoga* technique aims at controlling this pranic activity and direct it towards specific ends.

> 'The gross body is present in the waking state and absent in the state of dreaming, while *ātman* persists [is present in the two states]. The constant is the Self because in the state of dreaming, while It is present, the gross body is absent, therefore the latter is the variable factor'.

'In the same way the subtle body is absent in the state of deep sleep, while the *ātman* remains the unchanging witness. Thus while the Self persists in all states, the subtle body is not present in deep sleep, therefore it is the variable factor'.

'By understanding the nature of the subtle body, the *ātman* is detached from the sheaths of the *buddhi*, *manas* and *prāṇa* which are recognized as being different from the Self and composed of three *guṇas* in different proportions'.

'In the state of contemplation (*samādhi*) *avidyā*, in causal body form, no longer manifests itself, but the *ātman* is present. Thus *ātman* is the constant and the causal body becomes the variable factor'.

(*Pañcadaśī*: I, 38–39–40–41)

In short we have:

Prājña: *ātman* plus perception of *avidyā* (deep sleep)

Taijasa: *ātman* plus the oniric universe (dreaming)

Viśva: *ātman* plus the objective universe (waking)

Ātman is the factor common to all three states while perception and external objects vary from one state to another.

13. Certainly māyā has two powers: the projective one [vikṣepa-śakti] and the veiling one [āvṛti-śakti]. From the subtle body to the gross, all is created by the projective power.

The existence of the empirical world is the most stable and

lasting datum of perception, as a result it can not be denied. But in what do the three modes of existence we have seen above consist?

> 'The supreme Spirit is not born nor does it die, it comes from nowhere, it gives birth to nothing; without origin, permanent, eternal, ancient, it is not killed when the body is killed'.
>
> (*Kaṭha Up.*: I, II, 18)

Therefore, these states can not be the Absolute because This, being unconditioned, cannot become relative, the Non-born can not obviously be born, therefore what is it that we see and perceive?

When the nightly dreamer observes his universe as something external to himself, what does he perceive and experience? For him the dream is a real datum, just as the gross world is real to the waking person. We can not state that the data projected in the dream are the dreamer himself. He remains distinct, lying immobile and withdrawn. We can not take the effect for the cause, the object for the subject, the spectator for the spectacle. According to *Vedānta* the possibility of producing a phenomenon is due to *māyā*, which has the power of 'projecting' entire micro- and macrocosmic universes and then of 'veiling' and hiding the acting-non acting agent. *Vikṣepa-śakti* produces the projective phenomenon whereby the world of effects 'appears'; *āvṛti-śakti* intervenes so that the reflection of Consciousness of the unmoved con structor identifies with the apparent and phenomenal world. Hence comes *avidyā* and the 'ignorance-*fall*'. Identification with what we are really not, produces false perception with all its painful ensuing consequences.

Ego is the sum of objectified representations and tends to perpetuate that appearance and energetic aggregate so full of tendencies, impulses and dispositions. *Māyā* itself, on the other hand, exists and does not exist; when the dreamer resumes his absolute immobile condition of *Sat* [Existence] – which was never lacking but simply clouded over by *āvṛti-śakti* – *māyā* itself vanishes and disappears as if by magic. False mayahic perception makes us take the spectacle for the spectator, but as soon as Knowledge comes to our aid, that representation and that false idea of identity disappear without a trace.

> 'This visible universe has its roots on the mental plane, it vanishes when the mental element is resolved'.
>
> 'This *ātman* is neither the gross nor the subtle universe. As these two universes are but pure mental images, they have no reality, just as the snake we see where there is only a rope is not real – just as a dream is not real . . .'.
>
> 'From the Cosmic Intelligence (*Mahat*) to the gross body, all is the effect of *māyā*. This effect [the subjective-objective universe], with its Cause, *māyā*, is the non-Self; it is an illusion just like a mirage that appears in the desert'.
>
> '*Avidyā* or *māyā* [metaphysical, veiling Ignorance] also called the undifferentiated (*avyakta*) is the very power of the Lord [*Īśvara*].
> It exists since eternity; the three *guṇas* form it and, being the first cause, it is superior to all the consequent effects. Man, endowed with intelligence and mental clarity, is able, on the basis of these effects, to arrive at it by means of inference. Then he understands how he brought the whole universe into manifestation'.
>
> (Śaṁkara, *Vivekacūḍāmaṇi*: 407–246–123–108)

A similar philosophical vision can be found in Tibetan Lamaism. In the *Bardo Thödöl* (Tibetan book of the dead) a thesis is developed whereby the whole micro and macro-cosmic universe-spectacle (space-time) is a simple mirage-phenomenon produced by the projective power of the Dreamer-agent.

Sir James Jeans, English physicist, mathematician and astronomer, in *The New Background of Science* writes:

> 'We conclude that space means nothing outside of our perception of objects and that time also means nothing outside of our experience of events. Space begins to take on the fictitious aspect created by our minds, of an extension not proper to Nature, of a merely subjective concept which helps us to understand and describe the order of the objects as we see them; time, too seems fiction. The purpose of this pretence is the same: we need it, just like the fiction of space, to order the events that concern us'.

We can conclude that if time and space are considered by science as simple devices created by our minds, objects and events too become *ipso facto* simple mental creations, because their existence depends upon time-space.

14. In sat-cit-ānanda, nature of Brahman, the world of names and forms manifests itself just like the waves and spray which emerge from the ocean; this event is called manifestation.

From an empirical point of view we attribute the terms *sat*, *cit*, *ānanda* to *Brahman*, but *Brahman* is beyond all definition or qualification; being absolute, no attributive formulation can be assigned to It. The world of names and forms, we have seen, emerges from the projective thinking power of universal or human *jīva*, and *jīva* emerges from indirect Brahmanic participation. The nocturnal universe springs from the projective mental power of the Dreamer. The mind, in turn, is substance that moulds and is dynamically electrified by the power of *ātman*, as the electrons are electrified by the presence of the nucleus, while the nucleus remains the unaltered witness at the centre of the atom. One becomes what one thinks, because mental substance is the forger of things-events. Thus, what we call life emerges from the presence of *Brahman*, while This remains aloof in its absolute state. The common, objective material world – the spectacle – is only a 'condensed substantial idea' of the cosmic *Jīva*, and the subtle one is a more rarefied, less condensed, more brilliant, substantial idea.

If a difference exists, this is to be found in the various levels of materialization, condensation and in greater or less vibratory speed and intensity. The causal universe, both subtle and gross – the entire cosmic spectacle – is an *Image-Idea* at various vibratory levels. This concept is not absolute idealism because, we repeat, behind the Idea-Spectacle there is *Brahman*, the Absolute, substratum of this idea-phenomenon, just as behind the nocturnal ideal universe dwells the human thinker-dreamer, substratum of all, who, silent and solitary spectator, remains aloof, immobile and equidistant. *Vedānta* metaphysics is neither objective (because it does not consider the universe as real and self-sufficient) nor subjective (because the image-idea is taken to be a simple modification of the mental substance and the *jīva* itself is seen as a projection that is born and which dies just like any other phenomenon). *Brahman* is the substratum of all possible phenomena, therefore, of the whole of life, which we erroneously call objective and subjective, visible and invisible, inferior and superior, one and multiple.

15. The other power [of māyā, the veiling power] hides the distinction between the seer and the seen, situated within [the body], and that between Brahman and the world of appearances perceived outside [the body]. This power is the cause of the phenomenal universe.

The veiling power obliges the *jīva*'s reflection of consciousness – which originates from the *cit* of *ātman* – to consider itself as an object, to identify with its universe and become the prisoner of its own ideal projected web. This is why, during its nighly dreaming, the *jīva*-ego or the experimenter (creation of the mind) identifies with the imagined universe and rejoices or is troubled, according to whether each picture-event is pleasant or unpleasant. It has a life of its own, it moves, it feels various sentiments and has intuition of truths. It is only upon awakening, not before, that all this universe disappears and is recognized as a simple dream-mirage. Thus the veiling *māyā* hides the distinction between *Brahman* and the universe, between the Spectator and the spectacle. The two powers (*āvṛti-śakti* and *vikṣepa-śakti*) are born simultaneously. Wherever we find the one we find the other.

We must consider the fact that there are no changes or particularities in the One Reality, there are, however, various aspects of *māyā*-appearance.

16. Near the Witness [ātman], the mysterious body [the subtle, liṅga-śarīra body] identified with the gross body, is illuminated and, being animated by the reflection of Pure Consciousness, becomes operative individuality.

Jīva, and the modifications of thought, etc. are all born together. Obviously the analytical mind tries to further classify and subdivide the multiple, but at the same time the subject, the object and their reciprocal instrument of relationship appear. Similarly, in a dream, the experimenter and the picture-event-universe, the field of experience are all projected at one and the same time. *Jīva*, let us repeat, is the sense of individualized identity, as it is a 'separate and experimenting entity'. Its presence can be demonstrated by this sentence: I am distinct from all the others, I am *this* as opposed to *that*.

17. This, which has jīva's nature, appears as the effect of an illusory superimposition upon the Sākṣin-Witness. When the veiling power of māyā disappears then one can notice clearly the difference and, as a result, it [individuality] disappears.

'Before knowing *Brahman*, every being, being *Brahman*, is really identical to Totality. Just as mother-of-pearl may be mistaken to be silver and just as the sky is believed to be concave or blue, and so on, in the same way ignorance superimposes [upon a being's consciousness] the idea that he is neither *Brahman* nor the whole'.[1]

18. Similarly, under the influence of the veiling power that hides all distinction between the universe of appearances and Brahman, the Latter seems to possess the attributes of change of the former.

Just as the *ātman* from an individual point of view seems to have the qualifications of the vehicles of the *jīva*, so from a universal point of view, *Brahman* seems to possess those superimposed attributes belonging to the world of names and forms. When, for example, we erroneously superimpose the snake upon the rope, we give to the latter the snake's attributes and the rope, thus appears to possess characteristics that are not its own. To our sensorial eyes *Brahman* 'appears' now to be this, now to be that, but in reality the continuous and ceaseless changing of forms or of manifest life regards only the spectacle.

19. Even in this case the distinction between Brahman and the phenomenal world can be understood only when the veiling power of māyā has been eliminated. Thus change can be perceived in the manifestation and never in Brahman.

Let us recall that the cause of false mental representations

---

[1] Śaṁkara's commentary to the *Bṛhadāraṇyaka Up.*, I, IV, 10.

and of all erroneous identifications is *māyā*-ignorance, which, with its power, seems to cloud the consciousness-intelligence of the *jīva*; only with the sword of discrimination, of discernment and of superconscious intuition can the veiling power of *māyā*-ignorance be eliminated. Sleep, for example, darkens the individual's clear consciousness, it seems to deprive him of the complete and positive perceptive-intellectual vision he possesses; a similar veiling condition is, however, only relative and not absolute, because, upon waking, he resumes his conscious and intellectual entirety. A mist superimposes itself upon the *ātman*, like a cloud, hiding its total completeness; the *jīva*, thus conditioned, confounds all things, wanders through the world of samsaric conflict until, awakening to superconscious intuition, it discovers its true identity, its identity with *ātman*.

20. Existence [sat], shining Consciousness [cit] and Bliss [ānanda], name and form are the five universal characteristics; the first three refer to Brahman, the other two to the phenomenal universe [i.e. to the reflection].

The shining Consciousness is the symbol of all-illuminating intelligence and of consciousness-awareness. *Sat-cit-ānanda* is the very nature of *Brahman*, while the changing world of names and forms constitutes the great mayahic phenomenon of the Spectacle. A form, to whatever dimension it may belong, is a vibrant play of light-shadow that disappears almost as soon as it is born. The great cosmic symphony of shadows and lights unfolds in a throbbing of luminous, vibrating coils undergoing continual and perennial change.

21. Pure Existence [sat], Pure Consciousness [cit] and Pure Bliss [ānanda] are common not only to the ether [ākāśa], to the air, fire, water and earth, but also to the gods, men and animals; only names and forms [created by mental power] render one thing different from others.

This *sūtra* is very important because it gives us the key by which to understand many things.

First of all *Brahmā*, as Active Principle, is present in every part of the manifest dimension, in the smallest sub-atomic particle as in the great sun. From this point of view we can say it is immanent, but at the same time transcendent because it operates and acts only indirectly, aloof from any change, just as our sun is immanent and at the same time transcends the earth. It is the sun that penetrates, heats and gives life to everything on this planet, but at the same time it is outside the phenomenal interplay of earthly life. All emerges from the intrinsic, infinite possibilities of *Brahman* and every manifested thing, seen from the point of view of the *ātman*, has no distinction or differentiation because it is upon its substratum that phenomena can arise. A form is a simple fleeting energetic modification of light. What is it, then, that makes us create absolute distinctions and classifications? What is it that spurs us towards conflict, towards the struggle for the assertion of these distinctions?

All chemical compounds are mere electronic substance or undifferentiated energy; what makes us believe that the element iron must be *absolutely* distinct from gold and have a different value? All compounds, being unstable, therefore changeable, must slowly dissolve into the undifferentiated electronic substance whence they first emerged. There is no instant of time in which all manifest things do not undergo some process and change, going back towards their 'original' condition. How can we distinguish one electron from another? *Vedānta* says that the distinction, classification and crystallization of forms is carried out only by the sensory mind which is unable to penetrate the synthetic mystery of the One-without-a-second. The sensory mind crystallizes forms, and although a temporal product, wishes to *fix* the time-motion of the form, ignoring the fact that it is impossible to detain what by its very nature can not be restrained and crystallized. When we have just stated that a datum is, it has already changed. Man seems to want to capture and bridle time-space and does not realize that this desire makes him a prisoner. The infinite classifications, the numberless names, the possible differentiations are only an attempt by the sensory mind to give a definition to things, but it is inevitable that as soon as the definition emerges things have already changed.

That piece of metal which we are able to grasp can not have an eternal configuration because not even for one moment does it cease to transmutate. Forms are flashings that rend the fathomless darkness.

22. When one becomes indifferent to the world of names and forms and devoted to sat-cit-ānanda, one must practice Contemplation [samādhi] without interruption, concentrating either upon the centre of the Heart or upon an external seed thought.

When the disciple, with the sword of discrimination-discernment has separated the unreal from the Real, the finite from the Infinite, the phenomenon from the Noumenon, unstable appearance from True Immobility, superimposition from the Substratum, and has recognized that beyond every form and name the True *Brahman* exists, then he must forget what was known to him up to that moment and begin that meditation which will reveal what we might call, inadequately, the Substratum of the whole formal universe.

Thus we have the following realizative sequences:

1. The beginning of the process of distinction between subject and object, between observer and the observed (subject-object-subject, etc. sequence of perception).

2. The discernment that the spectacle is distinct from the observer.

3. The recognition of the fact that the spectacle is subject to change and therefore it appears to be in a continuous state of 'instability'. The great world of names and forms is a mirage which appears and disappears to sensory perception.

4. The recognition of the fact that the subject-agent, together with all other data, is itself a simple temporal product which has emerged from the homogeneous, one and indivisible Substratum, where not only all distinction between subject and object vanishes, but also that between the various experimenters, in whatever dimension they may happen to be.

At this point one must undergo the integral Realization of the *Brahman*-Substratum, no longer by means of the empirical mind – whose purpose has now been fulfilled – but by means of *samādhi* (a kind of superconscious awareness which is direct, while the analytical mind's awareness is only indirect), that is the only means by which to reveal the nature of the One-without-a-second.

So we have the following framework:

– *World of names and forms*

– *Subject-experimenter-jīva*
(with its operative instruments)

– *Ātman-Brahman-Witness*

23. In the centre of the Heart two kinds of samādhi can be practised: one in which ideas are present (savikalpa), the other in which ideas are absent (nirvikalpa). The first kind is subject to distinctions: it can be associated with an object of perception or with a sound [as object].

Samādhi is a state of being, a direct experimentation; it is learning removed from mental imagination, from intellectual intuition itself and from every form of inductive, deductive or synthetic speculation. *Samādhi* is not a hypnotic trance, it is not a paranormal power, therefore it is not telepathic or mediumistic sensitivity nor is it a phenomenon that can be traced back to the empirical individualized state.

Many paranormal phenomena are only extentions of the expressive potentialities of the ego within particular infra-individual dimensions. Many disciplines think that *Brahman* – the One-without-a-second, the Substratum without cause, without parts – can be perceived, analysed and conceptualized by means of simple sensory perception. Such an empirical procedure prolonged with insistence could lead to total bewilderment, at a pathological state or even to pointless agnosticism. To recognize that the sixth sense (the mind) is an inadequate and limited instrument just like the other five, is a necessary step in order to emerge from this inevitable *impasse* to which the mind, inevitably, leads. The Substratum can not be known through any of the sensory organs, otherwise it would not be the Substratum at all but a simple perceiveable object-phenomenon. We insist upon this point because all research must be undertaken with the appropriate tools and suitable modes of approach. In *savikalpa-samādhi* the consciousness experiences the global unity of multiple phenomena, but it is the very consciousness of *jīva*, which, finding itself in the differentiated state, continues to make subject-object distinctions. *Savikalpa* means literally 'with differentiation' and reveals the nature of the manifested world, while *nirvikalpa*, which means 'without differentiation', is the true brahmanic state of One-without-a-second where all distinction vanishes. The subject and the object disappear completely and the *jīva* merges into *That*.

> 'But the way is denied to us above all because the intelligence of that One is not attained either through knowledge or thought, as is the case with the other objects

of the Spirit, but only by means of a presence which is of greater value than knowledge . . .'.

(*Enneads*: VI, 9, IV.)

24. Desires, etc. centred in the mind are objects [of knowledge]. It is necessary to meditate upon Consciousness [cit] as the Witness of these mental modifications. This state is called savikalpa-samādhi – samādhi associated with an object (of knowledge).

A desire (see *śloka* 4) is always an object of perception that may be inhibited, satisfied, changed or transcended. This process reveals the existence of a centre of volition behind the object of knowledge. It is useful therefore to consider the internal object as a simple movement of thought with which we must not associate or identify. Here the object is internal-subjective.

Thus, we can place ourselves in a position of 'stillness' and *observe-perceive* all the possible psychic contents that may arise in the field of our consciousness. To observe means to become aware in a direct manner, not through the medium of conceptualization of the content; in other words it is necessary to avoid thinking process.

This implies having created a willful non-identification with the various enslaving energetic contents so as to render them mere *objects* of knowledge. Then we must fuse our attention with our consciousness so that the latter may remain in its pure state. Here all objects vanish.

25. I am sat-cit-ānanda, independent, self-resplendent, free from duality. This is known as [the second kind of] savikalpa-samādhi, associated with a [subjective] sound.

Sat, *cit* and *ānanda* are, from an empirical point of view, the characteristics of *ātman*. But we must recall the fact that *ātman* in its absoluteness has no qualities or attributes. We notice that in this kind of *samādhi* the object of contemplation shifts. Here the consciousness returns to itself as *sat-cit-ānanda*.

As regards the sound, it is necessary to point out that for *Vedānta* philosophy there is a precise connection between name and object, and that names are not the outcome of arbitrary connection. Modern scientific discoveries have shown the importance and the profundity of this truth. Every form-object is simply a combination of electro-magnetic vibrations, therefore, it follows that each one must have a precise colour and emit a particular sound. Every vibratory state is colour and sound at the same time. The atom is a pulsation of light and sound, and even thought itself is luminous, sound-producing geometry. To know the intimate vibratory combination of forms means to understand their harmonic structure, their true identity or their 'name'. The 'Word' is sound, and the Word of *Brahman* is *AUM*. *OM* (as it is pronounced) is the sound of power *par excellence* and its perfect resonance leads us on to the wavelength of *Brahman*. Meditation based upon the sound-*mantra*: '*Aham Brahmāsmi*' (I am *Brahman*) corresponds to the meaning of this *sūtra*.

26. Nirvikalpa-samādhi, on the other hand, is that in which the mind, like a flame protected from the winds, remains still. Here the disciple remains indifferent to and undisturbed by all external objects of meditation and even to internal objects associated with sound, because he is completely absorbed into the Bliss of Brahman.

In *nirvikalpa-samādhi* the mind finally finds stillness and total absence of thought, therefore of objects. The countless thought modifications of the mind cease and the *jīva* remains in the undisturbed serenity of the all-fulfilled. There is no internal or external object of meditation because the mind is devoid of perceptive content.

Let us propose again these analogies: to the individual state corresponds a universal state. The individual state belongs to the *jīva* (living soul), the universal state to *Īśvara*. Every *jīva* is closed within a particular world made of gross objective and ideal subjective conditions; the microcosm follows along the lines of the macrocosm. What occurs above occurs below and vice-versa. In the individual state we can distinguish the three conditions already indicated above:

Vaiśvānara = gross condition (waking)

Taijasa = subtle condition (dreaming)

Prājña = causal condition (deep sleep)

Of these three conditions the average individual usually knows only the gross; the *yogi*, on the other hand, not only knows the entire individual condition, but he elevates himself until he merges with the universal state. It is possible for him, therefore, through the various kinds of *samādhi* described above to understand successively:

Virāṭ
The totality of gross manifestation

Hiranyagarbha
The totality of subtle manifestation

Īśvara
The germinal causal state of macro and microcosmic manifestation

This means, furthermore, that the Liberated Being has shattered the chains of the ego and assumed a cosmic, universal consciousness, so that he no longer expresses himself in terms of 'I' and 'you', but in terms of Totality and Synthesis. In *nirvikalpa-samādhi* we may say there is no meditation, in the ordinary sense of the word, because there are no more objects upon which to meditate. In it *silence* establishes itself, which implies the end of psychic movement.

27. The first kind of samādhi [savikalpa] is possible using an internal [subjective] or external [objective] object. In this samādhi, the world of names and forms is dissociated from Pure Existence.

When we perceive a clay jar we notice two factors: one concerning its particular structural form, the other regarding its substance or the substratum from which it is made. The form is not absolute because it is changing, perishable, it is born, grows old and dies.

There is an indefinite number of jar-forms, but only one clay. We can concentrate upon the jar-form and identify with it to such a degree as to allow it to condition our entire existence. It is obvious, therefore, that – as it is an unstable, perishable, phenomenal and changeable item – sooner or later we will enter into conflict.

We may concentrate upon the essence and the substratum of the jar-form, that is upon the clay, and it is equally true that in this case we see the Eternal datum, a Constant, a Whole without parts, a Homogeneousness always equal to itself, therefore absolute. We can, therefore, meditate upon forms or upon the substratum that causes forms. We may, for example, concentrate upon countless changing and transforming chemical compounds or upon the self-generating undifferentiated electronic substance from which these phenomenal qualified compounds arise. Thus in *savikalpa-samādhi* one experiments the intimate structure, the internal correlation between forms and the Unity of the whole (the highest achievement of *savikalpa* is to become perfectly in tune with the Manifest One, *Īśvara*, the Creator of all forms, the great Cosmic *Jīva*, the Architect of that miracle we call the formal universe), while *nirvikalpa* transcends all formal appearance, all qualities and all *jīvas*, taking us directly to the Absolute Centre-Point, to the Substratum-Essence of all that was, is and will be.

It is necessary to make a distinction between the condition of deep sleep where names and forms disappear and *nirvikalpa-samādhi* where we have, it would seem at first glance, an analogous condition. In the state of deep sleep we remain in the causal body of the *jīva* (therefore still upon the manifest plane) at the germinal state; thus the perceptive phenomena disappear but their latent seeds, the initial cause of the phenomena, remain. The *jīva* is alone with its requests and its *karma* (action) at potential level, awaiting manifestation.

Therefore, the roots have not been cut off. In *nirvikalpa-samādhi* not only are names, forms, *karma* and even *jīva* itself absent, but also the countless individual, universal, micro and macrocosmic *jīvas*. Therefore one reaches a dimension beyond all phenomenon-manifestations and all subject-objects.

28. The Entity [Brahman] remains [always] of the same unconditioned nature and permeated by sat-cit-ānanda. The uninterrupted contemplation of this state is called mid-way reflection.

This is another *savikalpa* mode and is close to that described in *śloka* 25. The first *samādhi* incorporates an (internal) subjective idea, this one an (external) objective one. For *Vedānta*, Reality, in order to be such, must be an unchangeable and eternally valid 'constant', it must not depend upon other realities, upon anything but itself. All the rest is simple phenomenon, mirage, apparent movement.

On the basis of what has been said it is clear that *Vedānta* – making use of speculative considerations and direct and indirect experience – has arrived at the conclusion that the definition "Absolute Reality" can be attributed only to

Brahman. To attribute it to other apparent realities would mean that sooner or later we should have to modify our vision of life. Therefore, roughly speaking, the East, leaving aside partial or empirical truths, has pursued the quest for the Ultimate, Supreme, Absolute, Constant Reality.

Saint Augustine too states that the Ultimate Truth is unchanging:

> 'It really is because It is unchanging'.
>
> (*De Natura Boni*, 19)
>
> '. . . glance at the Unchanging Goodness'.
>
> (*C. Faust.*, XXII, 53)
>
> '. . . vision of the Unchanging Truth'.
>
> (*De Cons. Evang.*, I, 8]
>
> '. . . quest for the Unchangeable Truth'.
>
> (*Enarr. In. Ps.*, XLI, 7)
>
> '. . . Unchangeable Light'.
>
> (*Conf.*, VII, 16)
>
> 'The mind, judging visible things, knows it is superior to visible things. But when, due to its own progress and regression it knows itself to be changeable, it discovers above itself the Unchangeable Truth'.
>
> (*Lib. De Div. Quaest.*, LXXXIII, 45)
>
> 'Unchangeable Truth shines in the soul like a sun and the soul participates in Truth'.
>
> (*De Gen. C. Manich.*, I, 43)

With regard to *samādhi*-contemplation this is what Plotinus writes:

> '. . . As contemplation now ascends from Nature to the Soul and from the Soul to the Spirit; as contemplation becomes more and more intimate until it merges with the

contemplating subjects achieving total unity; as in the soul that has reached wisdom the matter of knowledge strives towards identity with the knowing subject as if anxious to become spirit; it is obvious that by now in this spirit, both subject and object will form a unity, but not in the sense of intimate appropriation, as in the case of better souls, but essentially because of and due to identity between being and thinking. As here there is no longer any difference between the one and the other, which if there were it would mean the existence at a higher level of another reality where no difference of any kind exists. Hence it is necessary that both be, in reality, a sole thing, but this means 'living contemplation', that is, contemplation where the object is not that which exists "in another". In fact, in the case where the object is in another, it is the other which is the living entity, the object is not a "living entity in itself" '.

(*Enneads*, III, 8, VIII)

One can note the contemplative ascendent sequence set down by Plotinus: perceptible nature (Body), intelligible nature (Soul) and spiritual nature (Spirit).

To understand Plotinus' terminology better we can relate it to that of *Vedānta*:

Vedānta	Plotinus
Brahman-Turīya	Unum-Bonum
Īśvara	Spirit
Hiranyagarbha	Soul
Virāṭ	Body

The three Plotinian hypostases (Spirit-Soul-Body) are considered here from the universal point of view. The universal *body*, and therefore individual particular bodies, are seen by Plotinus as a shadow, a reflection of the Universal Soul.

Here is an extract in which he suggests that we 'turn ourselves' into Light and Beauty:

'. . . Did you contemplate yourself, dwelling with yourself in pure solitude? Have you no impediment that causes you to lose Unity? Have you mixed nothing with yourself that prevents you from being truly and solely light? Light, I say, not measured in terms of size, not circumscribed by any outline that can enlarge or diminish it indefinitely. This light must be truly unmeasurable, greater than any measure and superior to any quantity. If you see yourself as having become so, that is a "vision", if you trust in yourself, while still down here below, you have reached the sublime and have no need of a guide to lead you, then fix your unfaltering gaze, because, alone, your eyes will behold great beauty. But if you present yourself at the vision rheumy-eyed and unpurified or weak-sighted you will be unable to bear, on account of the weakness of your eyes, the vision of such splendid objects and you will see nothing even if another points out to you the presence of what can be seen.

It is necessary that the observer become first like and similar to what must be seen and then apply himself to the vision. As the eye would never be able to see the sun if it did not become solar, so the soul can not contemplate Beauty without becoming itself beautiful. So, come! Let each one become god-like and beautiful if he wants to contemplate both God and Beauty'.

(*Enneads*: I, 6, IX)

29. The preceding [condition of) mental quiet is considered, on account of its Bliss, the third phase of samādhi. One must constantly achieve these six kinds of samādhi.

Here concentration upon an external object is described, while in *śloka* 26 concentration upon an internal-subjective one was described. According to this Treatise we have six kinds of *samādhi*: four *savikalpa* and two *nirvikalpa*. Here is a synthetic scheme of them:

SAMADHI LEVEL	SUBJECTIVE METHOD	OBJECTIVE METHOD
1st *savikalpa* phase	Any formal psychic content	Any external object
2nd *savikalpa* phase	Subjective sound Internal concept-Idea	Objective sound External concept – Idea
3rd *nirvikalpa* phase	Pure contemplation, devoid of any empirical subjective or objective support; direct contemplation of the *ātman* or of *Brahman*.	

30. By disidentifying with the body and realizing the supreme ātman, even if the mind is able to direct itself towards objects, one experiences (nirvikalpa) samādhi.

Following Vedantic teaching one arrives at an understanding of how the various body-sheaths or *upādhis* can not constitute that Supreme Absolute that is in all of us. Through discriminating analysis and consequent rejection of what can not be permanent Reality, the disciple frees himself from all the superimpositions that for a long time have kept him in error and bondage. The *jīva* identifies itself with all the sensations that come from outside and therefore states: I am happy, unhappy, rich, poor, this or that; the subject, therefore, adheres to the object and to its qualifications. These *ślokas* show that there is a difference between subject and object, between the spectator and the spectacle. When the disciple discriminates and recognizes that the spectacle is only a continuous flow of energy in countless forms that appear and vanish, he finally lets go of his attachment to the spectacle and reacquires his identity, his condition of rotation around his own axis. All sheaths, from the *buddhi* to the dense physical sheath are simply unstable, changeable energetic agglomerates which, as we have seen, make up the spectacle, that is, they are simply the objects of perception; therefore it is a mistake to identify with such phenomena and consider oneself an 'imprisoning, finite changeableness'. When, by ascesis, discrimination, meditation, etc., the *jīva* dissociates itself completely from the sheaths and recognizes the entire phenomenal energetic world as a simple, although marvellous, mirage of shades and light, standing out against the akashic screen of the infinite, then that event called *nirvikalpa-samādhi* may occur. Only in this state can we understand in all its true meaning the entire process of manifestation. The double *nirvikalpa-samādhi* refers to two direct data: *ātman* and *Brahman*. *Ātman* is associated with the *Persona* (in the Traditional sense) and *Brahman* with the Absolute as such; but *ātman* is only *Brahman* itself at certain levels of being.

31. When the chains of desire have been shattered, all doubts dispelled, all kinds of karma dissolved, 'That', which is both above and below [transcendent and immanent], is realized.

> 'The knot of desire is severed, all doubts are banished, the *karma* disappears when *That* which is at the same time transcendent and immanent is seen'.
>
> (*Muṇḍaka up.*: II, 3, 9)

That is beyond all polarity and therefore beyond all correlation. As long as we remain upon the mental plane of conceptual correlations, our consciousness simply experiences the mayahic world of evanescent, conflictual phenomena.

Here are the various correlations that must be overcome in order to reintegrate oneself with *That*:

Non-manifest	Manifest
Being	Non-being
Non-motion	Motion
Homogeneous-unity	Multiplicity
Universal	Particular
Subject	Object
Archetype	Prototype
Transcendence	Immanence
Aformal	Formal
Essence	Substance
Principial	Effectual
Idea	Expression
Noumenon	Phenomenon

That – Turīya – Brahman

With the achievement of *nirvikalpa-samādhi* all limitations and enslavements are transcended; there is no longer any obstacle or impediment that can hold back the liberated soul. In this state of perfect Identity there is nothing more to fulfill.

A *Jīvan-mukta* (Living Liberated Being) contemplates *Brahman* with open eyes 'in heaven, on earth and in every place'; for him there are no barriers against this total fulfilment, therefore all possible duality vanishes.

The various types of *karman* are:

- *Saṁcita-karman*: that is, that stored up in the past, still latent and yet to ripen;

- *Āgāmi-karman*: that built up during a lifetime, that is during one's present life;

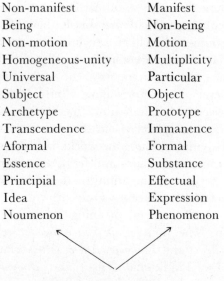

- *Prārabdha-karman*: that already matured and impossible to neutralize. For example, the gross physical body is the effect of *prārabdha-karman* and obviously must await its distintegration in order to dissolve that *karma*. However, even *prārabdha-karman* for the *Jīvan-mukta* is as if it were inexistent, because he has ceased to identify with it to such a degree as to consider himself bodyless.

'For the Sage who lives in his Own Self as *Brahman*, the One-without-a-second, and who no longer identifies with superimpositions, the question of knowing whether or not *prārabdha-karman* exists is senseless. Does he who awakens keep up the slightest relationship with the objects of his dream?'.

'The *prārabdha-karman* continues to have an effect only upon the ignorant who identify with their gross body. But no one can hold that the Knower of *Brahman* identifies with his body, therefore the *prārabdha-karman* hypothesis must be rejected'.

'Although [the *Jīvan-mukta*] acts he remains inactive; although he experiences the fruits of past actions, he is not touched by these.
Although he has a body of flesh he does not identify with it; although he is limited he is omnipresent'.

'Neither pleasure nor pain, nor good, nor evil can touch the Knower of *Brahman*. Although he goes on living in this objective world he is free even of the notion of body'.
(Śaṁkara: *Vivekacūḍāmaṇi*: 454, 460, 544, 545)

32. There are three types [conceptions] of jīva: the limited, the falsely presented and that imagined in dreams.

This aphorism is extremely important because it mentions

three theories regarding *jīva*. What is *jīva*? What is its nature? What is the difference between *Brahman*, *ātman* and *jīva*?

The first conception referred to in this *sūtra* is this: the *jīva* can be compared to the ether in a jar, which jar is the *upādhi*, that is the vehicle or the limiting body. This ether, although surrounded by the structure of the jar-form, is of the same nature as the free and unbound ether outside the jar.

The second conception can be compared to a ray of sun dancing on the water. The movement is caused by the water and not by the ray, but at first glance it is the ray that appears to be moving. Thus the ray of pure consciousness reflects upon the *buddhi* which moves as *jīva*.

The third conception of *jīva* may be compared to the experimenting subject of dreaming. The nocturnal *jīva*, or reflection of the individualized consciousness, experiences the various phenomena and qualifications inherent to its state: pleasure-pain, knowledge-ignorance, various types of desire, etc.

The first *jīva* is the result of limitations (*avacchedavāda*), the second and third are the outcome of objectivated reflections (*ābhāsavāda* and *pratibimbavāda*).

Jīva is, therefore, a projection of *ātman*, just as the molecule of a chemical element is a combinatorial, vibrating, electronic projection. And just as the hydrogen molecule is after all only an elementary or electronic particle, so too is *jīva* simpy *ātman*.

Jīva exists as long as *māyā-avidyā* lasts, which *māyā-avidyā* supplies the driving power that allows the *jīva* to survive. Thus the nocturnal *jīva* exists as long as the veiling *māyā*-dream lasts.

Jīva can move through endless possible experiences: negative and positive, harmonic or disharmonic, just as it can dissolve back into its atmic source.

With regard to *jīva*, Svāmi Siddheśvarānanda of the Rāmakṛṣṇa Order writes: 'In the *jīva* the principle of conscious activity is called *manas*, while the principle of non-conscious activity is called *prāṇa*. At every rebirth only the gross body is taken on. The other two, the subtle and the causal, which have survived previous death and which guarantee the continuity of individuality, associate with the new physical body. These three elements: gross body, *manas* and *prāṇa* form, in a certain way, the *jīva*'s empirical dwelling-place'.

Here is a scheme of what we have said:

Ātman = Personality

Jīva = Nucleus of individualized semipermanent life

Bodies = Instruments of relationship or contact

The empirical ego is merely the state of temporal-spatial life experienced during incarnation. The ego is one of the many possible actors that play certain parts upon the stage of the material-formal world or the outpost of the *jīva* upon a particular plane of existence.

Individuality, as *jīva*, has experienced and can still experience countless moments of transmigration at gross physical level and 'I am this' is its particular state at that moment. The ego-actor experiences qualifications rooted in the three prakritic *guṇas*.

The ego is the mask that the *jīva* wears when it exteriorizes itself upon the dense physical plane. Thus in the morning the ego-actor of dreams dissolves and with the dream of the next night (which on the plane of the *jīva* corresponds to another transmigratory experience) a new ego-actor is born to experience further individualized modes.

From this we infer that what comes and goes, what takes or does not take form is the *jīva*-individuality, not the *ātman*. From the point of view of the *ātman*, if one may say so, the *jīva* does not exist nor does it come or go.

From the point of view of the *ātman* every phenomenon, including the *jīva*, is simply 'apparent motion', and *māyā* represents this apparent motion, from the atmic point of view.

Realization consists in dissolving not only the ego of the moment but the *jīva*-individuality itself, the semipermanent 'atomic-nucleus' which is much more persistent and long-lasting than the momentary ego-actor. When the cause is removed at the source, the effect disappears as a result.

33. Limitation is illusory, but what appears to be limited is real. The jīva condition is due to superimpositions of attributes upon ātman, but This is of the same nature as Brahman.

Reality *appears* limited due to *māyā*. The metaphysical Unity seems to be manifold on account of *māyā*. Just as in a dream, the mind appears multiple (the varied universe of dream) due to the *māyā*-sleep veil.

Superimpositions make data appear different from what they are. When, for example, we project the image-form of a snake where there is simply a rope, it is obvious that the snake with all its qualifications superimposes itself upon an underlying reality, hiding it completely. This apparent image-form takes on a dimension and consistency and can only be removed when one becomes aware of the rope.

When, due to the intrinsic power of the *ātman*, the *jīva*-shadow takes on consistency with all its sheaths, the reflection of consciousness attributes to *ātman* the characteristics of the sheaths so that, apparently, the nature of Self is perverted and eluded. If we were to assign the attributes of the earth to the sun – which is the real life-giver – we would make the same mistake.

34. The vedic mantras 'Tat tvam asi' [That thou art], etc. state the Identity of jīva with Brahman without parts. This Identity is applied to the limited jīva [see sūtra 32] and not to the other two jīvas.

There are four *mantras* in the *Vedas* which assert the Identity of *jīva* with *Brahman*:

- *Tat tvam asi*: That thou art
- *Ayam atmā brahma*: This *ātman* is *Brahman*
- *Ahaṁ brahmāsmi*: I am *Brahman*
- *Prajñānam brahma*: Pure Consciousness is *Brahman*

We analysed the *Tat tvam asi mantra* in our commentary to Śaṁkara's *Vivekacūḍāmaṇi*. Here we can take up again some of the explanatory points.

In *Vedāntasāra*, chapter IX, we read:

> '. . . now the great utterance: "That thou art" must be understood. It explains the meaning of the connection between the visible and the invisible . . .
> In the sentence "This is the same Devadatta" the terms *this* and *the same* (which distinguish respectively between the Devadatta of preceding time and that of the present) are related because they belong to the same Devadatta; thus in the saying "That thou art" (which underlines the visible and the Invisible) the two terms are correlated by the fact that they refer to the same existential condition'.

If we take the element zinc and the element crystal we can consider them in opposition because they manifest a different condition, but if we eliminate the spatial-temporal superimpositions inherent in them we find a homogeneous electronic condition, their common substratum so that it is no longer possible to recognize any opposition or difference.

The method used to arrive at the affirmation of Identity is called *bhāga-tyāga-lakṣaṇā* and consists, in fact, in resolving the contradictions in a datum. Bared of all contradiction and therefore of all empirical dualism, Truth reveals itself in its undivided unity.

35. Projective and veiling māyā lies in Brahman. It, by covering the indivisible nature of Brahman, imagines the universe [jāgat] and the jīva.

For an explanation of *māyā* and its attributes see *śloka* 13 and its commentary. All that is manifest has, after all, its origin in *Brahman* because nothing can be outside of *Brahman.*

36. The false presentation of consciousness in buddhi, which operates various actions and gathers their fruits, is called jīva. What, on the other hand, consists in elements with their relative products which belong to the nature of enjoyment, is called universe [jāgat].

Jīva, as we have already seen, is the experimenter-actor which causes action, therefore *karma*, and gathers the good or bad fruits depending upon the direction given to its movements. The more it identifies with the physical, subtle and causal process, the more it wanders through the samsaric world; the more it is stimulated by this world, the more it is subdued and enslaved by interested translatory action. The buddhic reflection of consciousness imagines *jīva* as absolute *ātman*, while it is really only a simple phenomenon. The objective exterior world is its greatest attraction and its field of enjoyment and suffering. The five elements of which the phenomenal Universe is composed are: ether, air, fire, water, earth. These must not be mistaken for the chemical compounds of science. In reality, they are one sole element which in time becomes divided into two, three and finally four. Upon the four-fold division all the intimate structure of manifestation is based. Ether is *ākāśa* which pervades all, it is the 'cosmic egg' born from the mind of *Brahmā.*

37. These [jīva and jāgat], that have no beginning, exist only for whoever has not yet achieved Liberation. Therefore both are phenomenal.

Jīva and the universe itself return in a condition of latency to the third state of *prājña* (deep sleep) and disappear completely, dissolving away in the Fourth or *Turīya*. Both *jīva* and *jāgat* are effects, appearances showing continuously changing phenomenal activity. They are not real and absolute because they do not live a reality of their own; they appear and disappear down through eternity; on the other hand, they can not be considered totally illusory and non existent; we can say that they are simple phenomena which have an authentic and real substratum of their own: *Brahman*. A *Jīvan-mukta* has solved the problem of *jīva* and even of the *jāgat itself*.

The Liberated Being is not an entity with an ego, a name, a form, an individual activity or ideal; he is not an energetic compound opposed to other living compounds whatever their dimension. The Liberated Being, being fulfilled, complete and rotating around his own axis, carries out no further actions of any order or nature whatsoever, but he simply reveals himself; he innocently effuses his radiance.

We have seen above that it is the *jīva* which brings about actions and longs for gratification, the fruit of unsatisfied desires; it is the *jīva* which accepts or refuses, it is it which constantly judges, compares and conceptualizes, it is the *jīva* which performs good and evil, but when this *jīva*-individuality, by means of resolving brahmanic Realization disappears from the scene, of what acting or non-acting, of what attraction or repulsion, of what good or evil may one speak?

The *nirvikalpa samādhi* is the point at the Centre, the absolute Pole, the highest realization of being, that which reintegrates the fragmentary consciousness of the conflictual *jīva* with totality, that which resolves the knower, the known and knowledge.

38. Associated with an erroneous presentation of consciousness, torpor-sleep, which participates in projection and darkening, begins to cover [in the waking state] the jīva and the perceived universe; then [during dreams] it imagines further object-universes.

Here two conditions of *jīva*, waking and sleep with dreams, are singled out. We have to recall that *Vedānta* has adequately treated these three conditions (waking, dreaming and dreamless deep sleep) both from the psychological and the philosophical point of view. Gauḍapāda, the first codifier of *Advaita Vedānta* and the spiritual Master of Śaṁkara, commented on the *Māṇḍūkya Upaniṣad* with great acumen. This *Upaniṣad* describes, from a metaphysical-philosophical point of view, the above-mentioned three states. Each state possesses a peculiar mode of consciousness of its own, different from the others.

We consider the waking state to be real and the dreaming state, as well as any other possible subtle subjective state, to be illusory because we identify with the reference frame of the waking state. But how can we judge one expression of life from the point of view of a different one?

Every set of co-ordinates has its own laws and mechanisms and, if we want to handle the problem of the truthfulness of that system, we must keep to its laws and modalities.

To carry out comparisons and assessments upon the basis of relationships is possible and useful, but one cannot judge or formulate truths based upon particular, limited time-space points of view. Thus a dream may be considered non-real only if judged from the point of view of waking, that is from another frame of reference.

Those who have experienced the state of *prājña* hold that both the subtle state, which in analogy is represented by dreaming, and the gross waking state are illusory, that is non-real.

Hence the *Vedānta* admonition to experiment certain systems of co-ordinates before stating and judging.

By means of various kinds of *samādhi* the individual can well experience reference systems that transcend the physical-gross (*viśva-virāṭ*) order.

The common man, but even the scientist (more the latter than the former, in fact) considers the waking state as the only absolute reality in an *a priori* fashion, but this statement is arbitrary.

On the other hand, according to *Vedānta*, to state that the objects perceived during waking, dreaming and deep sleep are simple phenomena, one must 'really' achieve the Fourth or *Turīya* state. Only then can we find in each of the three individual and universal states, the unvarying, the constant and pure Consciousness-Existence.

Only this Realization of truth gives us the right to consider as 'dreams' the experiences of the universal condition. Simple intellectual conviction is only a preliminary phase. *Vedānta* metaphysics, more than a conceptual system attempting to prove something, is above all 'experience', 'transfiguration' of the entire psycho-physiological component, it is ascension and fulfilment of *nirvikalpa-samādhi*.

39. They [the subject and object of perception] are both illusory because they exist only as long as the experience [of dreaming] lasts. In fact, no dreaming jīva, once it has woken up again, ever sees the same objects in another dream.

The whole spectacle exists only in the gross, subtle and causal-germinal condition. Now, as we said before, we think that only what is in the gross state is real because it is more stable and material. But, in actual fact, there is never a moment when the physical world undergoes no change or atomic or molecular transformation.

A star is born, grows, matures, gets old and dies, and these events are an uninterrupted flow of change. If we agree that the Absolute must be eternally 'constant', 'unvarying' then we can not look for it in the world of phenomena, whether objective or subjective.

'No person is certain, unless he takes it on faith, of when he wakes or sleeps, seeing that during sleep, he believes himself more awake than he is when waking. He recognizes space, images, movements; he perceives the passage of time and measures it, and acts in the same way as he does when awake. As half of our life is spent asleep, and that is a matter of fact, and as what appears to us during it is not at all true, as everything we feel is illusion, who knows if the other half, when we are awake and thinking, is not a kind of sleep different from the first . . . thus weaving dreams upon dreams?'

(Pascal: *Thoughts*)

We may add that the consciousness experiences different systems of co-ordinates and holds to be real that particular system to which it gives its attention and in which it places its experience of life. When, however, it reintegrates itself with the One-without-a-second, it discovers that the various systems of co-ordinates have disappeared because, in reality, they were only manifestations of its own projective power.

40. The jīva of dreams considers the world that is dreamt to be real, but the empirical jīva [of waking] considers it to be unreal.

The universe of dreaming is real to the dreamer just as much as the objective one is to him when he is in the waking state. The dreaming *jīva* suffers, rejoices, acts and experiences states of consciousness just as much as the waking one, and it realizes it has dreamed only when it awakens. Thus, in the state of waking the object and the subject of dreams are unreal.

41. The objective jīva [viśva] considers this world of waking as being just as real, but the true jīva [ātman] understands that such a world is not at all real.

Just as the dreaming *jīva*, examined above, considers its nocturnal universe to be real so too the empirical objective *jīva* considers the daytime universe real; however, the true *jīva*(*ātman*) considers both these universes as unreal. In reality it is the same *jīva* which experiences the waking, dreaming and deep sleep states, thus it is the witness of the three states and the prisoner of the five sheaths; but beyond these three states exists the unconditioned *ātman* where the empirical experimenter loses himself. These states, let us repeat it, must not be investigated only by reason and analysis, but lived and experienced.

42. The true jīva recognizes the fact that his Identity with Brahman is Real and sees nothing besides this Identity. All the rest he considers illusion.

The *jīva*, by freeing the consciousness from the continual flow of formal energy and from the objectivating thought-flow itself, discovers that there is a substantial difference between the spectator and the spectacle. The effective achievement of the 'Metaphysical immobility' of the Self (Non-action) causes a detached contemplation of the continually changing mobility (action) of the triple objective sphere. In order that the *jīva* may become the *autonomous* observer of the entire force field, it must necessarily render itself 'Immobile' amid the 'mobile'. As long as it flows with the forces and through them, identifying itself with them, it can not either dominate or transcend them.

> 'In It there is no plurality whatsoever. He who sees multiplicity in It [*Brahman*] simply passes from one death to another'.
>
> 'That second thing is not . . .'.

'Therefore, this description [of *Brahman*] follows: not this, not this'.

(*Bṛhadāraṇyaka up.*: IV: IV-19, III-23; II: III-6)

'There is only One who has no second'.

'The difference consists only in the name coming from discourse'.

'It [*Brahman*] is neither gross nor subtle, neither short nor long. It is devoid of sound, of form and is unchanging'.

(*Chāndogya up.*: VI: II-1, I-5)

'Indra [the Supreme Lord] through *māyā* assumes different forms'.

(*Ṛg Veda*: VI, XLVII, 18)

43–44. Just as taste, freshness and fluidity, the attributes of water, seem to belong to the waves and then to the spray, of which the waves are the substratum, so too Absolute Existence, Consciousness and Bliss [which are of the Witness], seem to belong to the jīva of waking and dreaming experiences.

The whole empirical world seems to possess absolute existence and consciousness because behind it lies the Substratum which is always identical to itself. Thus the gross body seems to possess the characteristics of existence and sensitivity because it has in it that vital force which makes it active and vibrant. We must not take cause as being effect.

45. When drops of foam go back to being waves, fluidity, freshness, etc., they dissolve into the waves, and then in turn the waves dissolve into the ocean.

Spray of water, waves of all sizes whatsoever etc. are simply phenomena of the ocean in movement, shifting of its molecules; beyond these contingent phenomena only one unique reality exists: the ocean always equal to itself.

Here are a number of passages from Plotinus which show the unity that exists between the Soul and the Metaphysical One:

> 'When the Soul has the good fortune of reaching it, when He [the One] comes to the Soul, or better still, reveals his presence as soon as the Soul has turned itself away from present things and prepares itself to be as beautiful as possible, and even reaches a likeness – the preparation and the type of ornamentation, I do not know how, become clear to those who prepare themselves – behold the Soul sees in itself Him who recently appeared, and between the Soul and God nothing more can stand, nor can they remain any longer two, but become one and the Other a sole thing . . .'.
>
> (*Enneads*: VI, 7, XXXIV)

> '. . . rather he belongs to Him and unites with Him and, as it were, he makes himself coincide with Him point upon point; and here below when two points coincide they become one, and if they separate they become two again. Thus, we too, for the moment speak of the One as something different. In fact, how can one speak of Him as of something different, when whoever saw Him did not see Him as different during contemplation, but saw Him as one with himself?'.
>
> (*Enneads*: VI, 9, X)

> 'Now, as they were not two, but the seer himself was a sole thing with the object seen (not "seen" but "united to"), whoever becomes thus, when fused with Him, were he able to remember the experience would possess within himself the image of Him. But as he was already one in itself at that moment he did not keep within himself any sense of differentiation, either with regard to himself or other

things, because there was no motion within him; no animosity, no desire for anything, because he had ascended the heights, and there was neither reason nor thought because even he himself did not exist, if one must say such an absurdity! [With the realization of the One, the Soul or the Seer, as simple reflections of light, dissolve into the One, becoming the One again, transcending the samsaric motion and all thought of the knowable]. And almost enraptured or inspired, he entered silently into isolation [*kaivalya*, according to *sūtra* 34, book IV of Patañjali's *Rāja-yoga*] and in a state which does not know shocks nor enclines away from His being and does no more retire into himself, remaining completely still, almost transformed into immobility itself.

Even beautiful things he has by now overcome; rather he rides above beauty itself, beyond the chorus of virtues [he is, namely, beyond positive or negative classification, beyond quantity, beyond Being itself which is, in fact, the primary qualification]: he is like one who, having penetrated inside the impenetrable sanctuary, leaves behind himself the stark statues of the temple . . . Even if he does not enter, if he thinks that the sanctuary is something invisible, the Font and the Principle, he will know that only the Principle sees the Principle, and that only similar with similar can merge; and he will not overlook anything of that divine content which his soul manages to enclose within itself, even before the vision; the rest he will expect of the vision itself. The rest, that is, for whosoever has overcome all, is He who preceeds all . . . Therefore, if anyone sees himself as already transformed into Him, he possesses within himself the similitude of Him, and if he passes from himself, i.e. from copy to the original, he has already reached the end of his journey [with the realization of Identity with *That*, the *jīva*-soul's journey has reached its end]'.

(*Enneads*: VI, 9, XI)

46. When the jīva of the dream experience is absorbed by that of waking, the existence, consciousness and the bliss of the nocturnal jīva dissolves into the waking state. When the jīva of the waking experience is absorbed by the Spectator-Witness, even its reflections of existence, consciousness and bliss dissolve into the Spectator-Witness.

When we state that the waking and dreaming condition are mental projections or modifications there are a number of important considerations we must not forget. We must always distinguish between the position of the individual *jīva* and that of the universal *Jīva* or *Īśvara*, the first cause of all manifestation, from the microcosm to the macrocosm. We can eliminate this duality only through Realization of the Fourth state: *Turīya*. The universe is a modification of the universal mind. This modification or projection takes on for the ego-individual or separate consciousness an 'objective' (dual), more stable character, let us say, apparently longlasting and the same for all, whereas our nocturnal individual projection is valid only for ourselves and less permanent.

From the individual point of view, the entire mental or subtle body is absorbed by the germinal state of deep sleep: *prājña*; from the universal point of view the entire cosmic mind, including the individual causal body, is absorbed into the germinal condition of *Īśvara*. Beyond both *jīvas*, individual and universal, there exists a common basis for both of them: *Brahman*, the Absolute-without-a-second. Between the compound iron and pure carbon there exists a vast difference on the plane of appearances; it is only when we go beyond compounds that we notice that there is a sole undifferentiated electronic substance at the basis of all, as the causal and virtual body of all future molecular differentiation. The *jīva* represents a separate consciousness, a scale of values, on the plane of appearances only, so that there are more or less perfect *jīvas*, or rather, more or less veiled forms of *māyā*. Śaṁkara's concept of realization rests exclusively upon a metaphysical and therefore brahmanic vision; therefore, it follows that all *jīvas*, great or small, more or less perfect, and the whole manifestation are merely light-shadows or mirages thrown upon the screen of Infinite *Brahman*.

The entire manifest dimension contains countless orders of consciousness or entities that go from the sub-human to the super-human and divine. The highest, even in the divine hierarchy, is still only a 'state of consciousness', however elevated it may appear to be to the humble eye of the human *jīva*. But all these *qualified* orders and degrees, those entities which have attributes and formal expression, disappear when seen from the metaphysical point of view of the Absolute *Brahman nirguṇa* (without attributes) revealed by Śaṁkara. The path of shamkarian *Advaita*, of the One-without-a-second, is the most difficult and the one which contains most snares; it is also the highest and most challenging that the human mind has ever known. All other *darśanas* and the two currents of *Vedānta* itself, that of Madhva (Dualism) and that of Rāmānuja (mitigated Monism), are based essentially upon the point of view of the First Cause: *Īśvara*, and therefore, are dualist or monist.

When studying and meditating upon *Advaita Vedānta* we have to keep these considerations in mind and, while carrying out our *sādhanā*, we should learn how to keep still at the centre of our own psychophysical system, becoming tempered in order to face all obstacles of *avidyā* at individual level and of *māyā* at universal level.

We should like to end these notes of commentary with the following words by Plotinus:

> 'If you manage to grasp it, having removed from it even being itself [the Principal One and Universal Spirit] you will fall into amazing stupor. Then reach out towards Him [*That* in *Vedānta*] and join Him in his dwelling-place, in peaceful restfulness: obtain an increasing sense of Him as

you become aware of Him by means of intuition and, although attracted towards things which come after Him and which owe Him their existence [the world of names and forms], take in His greatness at a glance'.

(*Enneads*: III, 8, x)

Transliteration of the Sanskrit text

Rūpaṁ dṛśyaṁ locanaṁ dṛk taddṛśyaṁ dṛktu mānasam |
dṛśyā dhīvṛttayassākṣī dṛg eva na tu dṛśyate || 1 ||

Nīlapītasthūlasūkṣmahrasvadīrghādibhedatah .
nānāvidhāni rūpāṇi paśyellocanamekadhā || 2 ||

Āndhyamāndyapaṭutveṣu netradharmeṣu caikadhā .
saṁkalpayenmanaḥ śrotratvagādau yojyatāmidam || 3 ||

Kāmaḥ saṁkalpasaṁdehau śraddhā 'śraddhe dhṛtītare .
hnīrdhīrbhirityevamādīn bhāsayatyekadhā citiḥ || 4 ||

Nodeti nāstametyeṣā na vṛddhiṁ yāti na kṣayam .
svayaṁ vibhātyathānanyād bhāsayet sādhanaṁ vinā || 5 ||

Cicchāyā ''veśato buddhau bhānaṁ dhīstu dvidhā sthitā .
ekāhaṁkṛtiranyā syādantaḥkaraṇarūpiṇī || 6 ||

Chāyā 'haṁkārayoraikyaṁ taptāyaḥpiṇḍavanmatam .
tadahaṁkāratādātmyāddehaścetanatāmagāt || 7 ||

Ahaṁkārasya tādātmyaṁ cicchāyādehasākṣibhiḥ .
sahajaṁ karmajaṁ bhrāntijanyaṁ ca trividhaṁ kramāt || 8 ||

Saṁbandhinossatornāsti nivṛttissahajasya tu .
karmakṣayāt prabodhācca nivartete kramādubhe || 9 ||

Ahaṁkāralaye suptau bhaveddeho apyacetanaḥ .
ahaṁkāravikāsārdhassvapnassarvastu jāgaraḥ || 10 ||

Antaḥkaraṇavṛttiśca citicchāyaikyamāgatā .
vāsanāḥ kalpayet svapne bodhe 'kṣairviṣayān bahiḥ || 11 ||

Mano ahaṁkṛtyupādānaṁ liṅgamekaṁ jaḍātmakam .
avasthātrayamanveti jāyate mriyate tathā || 12 ||

Śaktidvayaṁ hi māyāyā vikṣepāvṛtirūpakam .
vikṣepaśaktirliṅgādibrahmāṇḍāntaṁ jagat sṛjet || 13 ||

Sṛṣṭirnāma brahmarūpe saccidānandavastuni .
abdhau phenādivat sarvanāmarūpaprasāraṇā || 14 ||

Antardṛgdṛśyayorbhedaṁ bahiśca brahmasargayoḥ .
āvṛṇotyaparā śaktissā saṁsārasya kāraṇam || 15 ||

Sākṣiṇaḥ purato bhāti liṅgaṁ dehena saṁyutam .
citicchāyāsamāveśājjīvassyādvyāvahārikaḥ || 16 ||

Asya jīvatvamāropāt sākṣiṇyapyavabhāsate .
āvṛtau tu vinaṣṭāyāṁ bhede bhāte 'payāti tat || 17 ||

Tathā sargabrahmaṇośca bhedamāvṛtya tiṣṭhati .
yā śaktistadvaśād brahma vikṛtatvena bhāsate || 18 ||

Atrāpyāḥṛtināśena vibhāti brahmasargayoh .
bhedastayorvikārassyāt sarge na brahmaṇi kvacit || 19 ||

Asti bhāti priyaṁ rūpaṁ nāma cetyaṁśapañcakam .
ādyatrayaṁ brahmarūpaṁ jagadrūpaṁ tato dvayam || 20 ||

Khavāyvagnijalorvīṣu devatiryaṅnarādiṣu .
abhinnāssaccidānandāḥ bhidyate rūpanāmanī || 21 ||

Upeksya nāmarūpe dve saccidānandatatparaḥ .
samādhiṁ sarvadā kuryāddhṛtaye vā 'thavā bahiḥ || 22 ||

Savikalpo nirvikalpaḥ samādhirdvividho hṛdi .
dṛśyaśabdānuvedena savikalpaḥ punardvidhā || 23 ||

Kāmādyāścittagā dṛśyāstatṣākṣitvena cetanam .
dhyāyeddṛśyānuviddho 'yaṁ samādhissavikalpakaḥ || 24 ||

Asaṁgassaccidānandassvaprabho dvaitavarjitaḥ .
asmīti śabdaviddho 'yaṁ samādhissavikalpakaḥ || 25 ||

Svānubhūtirasāveśād dṛśyaśabdāvupekṣya tu .
nirvikalpassamādhissyānnivātasthitadīpavat || 26 ||

Hṛdīva bāhyadeśe 'pi yasmin kasmiṁśca vastuni .
samādhirādyassanmātrānnāmarūpapṛthakkṛtiḥ || 27 ||

Akhaṇḍaikarasaṁ vastu saccidānandalakṣaṇam .
ityavacchinnacinteyaṁ samādhirmadhyamo bhavet || 28 ||

Stabdhībhāvo rasāsvādāttṛtīyah pūrvavanmataḥ .
etaissamādhibhiṣṣaḍbhirnayet kālaṁ nirantaram || 29 ||

Dehābhimāne galite vijñāte paramātmani .
yatra yatra mano yāti tatra tatra samādhayaḥ || 30 ||

Bhidyate hṛdayagraṁthiśchidyante sarvasaṁśayāh .
kṣīyante cāsya karmāṇi tasmin dṛṣṭe parāvare || 31 ||

Avacchinnaścidābhāsastṛtīyaḥ svapnakalpitaḥ .
vijñeyastrividho jīvastatrādyaḥ pāramārthikaḥ || 32 ||

Avacchedaḥ kalpitassyādavacchedyaṁ tu vāstavam .
tasmin jīvatvamāropād brahmatvaṁ tu svabhāvataḥ || 33 ||

Avacchinnasya jīvasya pūrṇena brahmaṇaikatām .
tattvamasyādivākyāni jagurnetarajīvayoḥ || 34 ||

Brahmaṇyavasthitā māyā vikṣepāvṛtirūpiṇī .
āvṛtyākhaṇḍatāṁ tasmin jagajjīvau prakalpayet || 35 ||

Jīvo dhīsthacidābhāso bhavedbhoktā hi karmakṛt .
bhogyarūpamidaṁ sarvaṁ jagat syādbhūtabhautikam || 36 ||

Anādikālamārabhya mokṣāt pūrvamidaṁ dvayam .
vyavahāre sthitaṁ tasmādubhayaṁ vyāvahārikam || 37 ||

Cidābhāsasthitā nidrā vikṣepāvṛtirūpinī .
āvṛtya jīvajagatī pūrve nūtne tu kalpayet || 38 ||

Pratītikāla evaite sthitatvāt prātibhāsike .
na hi svapnaprabuddhasya punassvapne sthitistayoḥ || 39 ||

Prātibhāsikajīvo yastajjagat prātibhāsikam .
vāstavaṁ manyate 'nyastu mithyeti vyāvahārikaḥ || *40* ||

Vyāvahārikajīvo yastajjagadvyāvahārikam .
satyaṁ pratyeti mithyeti manyate pāramārthikaḥ || *41* ||

Pāramārthikajīvastu brahmaikyaṁ pāramārthikam .
pratyeti vīkṣate nānyadvīkṣate tvanṛtātmanā || *42* ||

Mādhuryadravaśaityāni nīradharmāstaraṅgake .
anugamyātha tanniṣṭe phene 'pyanugatā yathā || *43* ||

Sākṣisthāssaccidānandāsaṁbandhādvyāvahārike .
taddvāreṇānugacchanti tathaiva prātibhāsike || *44* ||

Laye phenasya taddharmā dravādyāssyustaraṅgake .
tasyāpi vilaye nīre niṣṭhantyete yathā purā || *45* ||

Prātibhāsikajīvasya laye syurvyāvahārike .
tallaye saccidānandāḥ paryavasyanti sākṣiṇi. || *46* ||

Bibliographical Appendix

We wish to give here a list of titles which those who desire to further their knowledge of the *Vedānta* doctrine may consult.

The choice is not easy because many writers who down through the ages made important contributions to the discussion of the doctrine can not be mentioned here. However our thanks and appreciation goes also to those we are unable to name here.

We shall divide the bibliography into three sections:

a) works that Raphael has consulted with regard to his Italian-language translations of Vedantic texts,

b) translations of the *Upaniṣads*, of the *Brahma-sūtra* and of the *Bhagavad-Gītā*,

c) studies, essays and monographs writing concerning *Vedānta*.

First of all it is necessary to clarify a number of points which should have been made in the first edition of this book, and which were later made in the *Vidyā* magazine.

– Raphael, rather than being an individual, represents a 'Group' and the work carried out is done by the 'Group' (the ashramic *Vidyā* group). Raphael has his specific task and functions within the 'Group'.

– The only aim of the ashramic group is to present the *Advaita* vision to those who are ready to 'spread their wings'.

Those who are ready for this experience do not need elaborate or intricate reasonings or erudite treatises. The attentive disciple needs only a 'vision' to meditate upon and *contemplate*.

To consider the *Vedas*, the *Upaniṣads*, the *Qabbālāh*, the philosophy of Pythagoras, Plato and Plotinus, etc. as mere intellectual playthings means betraying the purpose for which these texts were written and handed down to us. One must grasp the essence of a *sūtra* in order to meditate upon it and then embody it. After which the *sūtra* or the idea, the concept or the text, etc. may be thrown away because they have served their purpose as a stepping-stone. At this point it is opportune to quote some concepts by P. Priorini which were made in connection with the review of a book: '. . . it is useless to engage in intellectual, dialectical masturbation when reading Tao, or Zen or Buddhism (and we add *Vedānta Advaita*) if one is not prepared to accept the ultimate consequences and enter into the spiritual context which characterizes them, and which alone can reveal their true essence. If one is not prepared to take this final step then Freud is a useful alternative'. (From: *Il Minotauro* – Year III, Vol. I, May 1976).

Union and Identity with *That* can not occur upon rational bases or through intellectual knowledge. To want to construct a rational basis upon which to place the Ultimate Reality means simply speculating upon mental projections.

The Supreme Reality is 'evident' to that consciousness which has 'stripped' itself of all intra-individual emotions, concepts, and will.

– Some times it may happen that the literal translation of a *sūtra* is not given and what we consider to be a traditional interpretation is given instead. In such cases the spirit rather than the letter appears to us to be more appropriate.

– It may happen that the Sanskrit words appear with

articles and adjectives that do not take the original gender of the Sanskrit nouns into consideration: for example nouns referring to inanimate objects will become neuter in English whereas in Sanskrit they may be masculine or feminine.

– Not all the Vedantic texts will be translated by us as the Editrice *Āśram Vidyā* has narrowed down its choice to specific topics. Besides, the company which is a sector of *Associazione Āśram Vidyā*, is a non-profit-making organization.

– Those who for various reasons, other than commercial ones, wish to write or speak about the topics treated here may quote freely from the texts because Knowledge must be free from the concept of possession or property, whether material or psychological.

If the Editor reserves copyright, this is only with a view to offering an absolute guarantee of the integrity and originality, as well as the continuity, of the works and therefore of the Doctrine.

a) *Works that Raphael has consulted with regard to his Italian-language translations of Vedantic texts:*

Chidbhavānanda, *The Bhagavad Gītā*, Śrī Rāmakrishna Tapovanam Publication Section, 1974.

Gambhirānanda Svāmi, *Eight Upaniṣads*, 2 vols., Advaita Āshrama, Calcutta 1956.

Gamḅhirānanda Svāmi, *Brahma-Sūtra Bhāṣya of Śaṅkarācārya*, Advaita Āshrama, Calcutta 1972.

Guenon R., *L'uomo e il suo divenire secondo il Vedānta*, Edizioni Studi Tradizionali, Torino 1964.

Guenon R., *Introduzione generale allo studio delle dottrine indù*, Edizioni Studi Tradizionali, Torino 1965.

Lacombe O., *L'Absolu selon le Vedānta*. Geuthner, Paris 1966.

Mahadevan T.M.P., *The Philosophy of Advaita*. Vedānta Pr., London 1938.

Mahadevan T.M.P., *Śaṁkarācārya*, National Book Trust, New Delhi 1968.

Morretta A., *Il pensiero Vedānta*. Abete, Roma 1968.

Müller M., *The Upanishads*, 'Sacred Books of the East', vols. I and XV, Motilal Banarsidass, reprint Delhi 1969.

Nikhilānanda Svāmi, *The Upanishads*, 4 vols., Phoenix House, London 1951–59.

Nikhilānanda Svāmi, *The Māṇḍūkyopanishad with Gauḍapāda's kārikā and Śaṁkara's commentary*, Śrī Rāmakrishna Āshrama, Mysore 1968.

Radhakrishnan S., *The Bhagavad Gītā*, Allen and Unwin, London 1948.

Radhakrishnan S., *The Brahma-Sūtra*, Allen and Unwin, London 1960 (reprint of 1960, Greenwood 1968).

Radhakrishnan S., *The Principal Upaniṣads*, Allen and Unwin, London 1974.

Sauton M., *Le plus beau fleuron de la Discrimination, Vivekacūdāmani par Śrī Śaṁkarācārya*, A. Maisonneuve, Paris 1964.

Siddheśvarānanda Svāmi, *Quelques aspects de la philosophie vedantique*. A. Maisonneuve, Paris 1941–42.

Siddheśvarānanda Svāmi, *La meditation selon le yoga Vedānta*, A. Maisonneuve, Paris 1955.

Siddheśvarānanda Svāmi, *Pensée indienne et mystique carmélitaine*, Centre védantique Rāmakrishna, Gretz 1974. Traduzione italiana *Pensiero indiano e Mistica carmelitana*, Edizioni Āśram Vidyā, Roma 1977.

Thibaut G., *The Vedānta Sūtras with the commentary of Śaṅkarācārya*, Sacred Books of the East, vols. XXXIV, XXXVIII, Motilal Banarsidass, Delhi reprint 1968.

Āśram Vidyā are indebted to several eminent authorities, whom they wish to thank sincerely for their valuable contributions, particularly Svāmi Nikhilānanda, Gambhirānanda and Siddheśvarānanda, of the Rāmakṛṣṇa Order.

b) *Translations of the* Upaniṣads *of the* Brahma-sūtra *and of the* Bhagavad-Gītā:

Upaniṣads

Aiyar N.K., *Thirty Minor Upanishads*, Madras 1914.
Aurobindo Sri, *Trois Upaniṣads (Īśa, Kena, Muṇḍaka)*, Michel Albin, Paris 1972.
Aurobindo Sri, *The Upanishads*, Pondicherry 1972.
Bhaktivedanta Svāmi Prabhupāda, *Śrī Īśopaniṣad*, Bhaktivedanta Book Trust, (traduzione italiana) 1975.
Belloni-Filippi F., *Due Upanishad: la dottrina arcana del bianco e del nero Yajurveda*, Carabba, Lanciano 1912.
Belloni-Filippi F., *Kaṭhaka-upaniṣad*, Orsolini-Prosperi, Pisa 1905.
Böhtlingk O., *Bṛhadāraṇyakopanishad* (*Mādhyaṁdina* review), Kaiserliche Akademie der Wissenschaften, St. Petersburg 1889.
Böhtlingk O., *Khāndogyopanishad*, Haessel, Leipzig 1889.
Bousquet J., *Praśna Upanishad*, 'Les Upanishad' vol. VIII, A. Maisonneuve, Paris 1948.
Buitenan van J.A.B., *The Maitrāyaṇīya Upaniṣad*, 'S-Gavenhage, 1962.
Cowell E.B., *Kauṣītaki Upaniṣad* 'Bibliotheca Indica', Calcutta 1901 (reprint 'Chowkhamba Sanskrit Series', 64, Benares 1968).
Cowell E.B., *Maitrāyaṇīya Upanishad*, 'Bibliotheca Indica', Asiatic Society, n. 1368, Calcutta 1935.
Della Casa C., *Upaniṣad*, Utet, Torino 1976.
Deussen P., *Sechzig Upanishad's des Veda*, reprint Darmstadt 1963.
Elenjimittam A., *Le Upaniṣad, Isa, Katha, Mundaka, Mandukkya*, Mursia 1980.
Esnoul A.M., *Maitrāyaṇīya Upanishad*, 'Les Upanishad' vol. XV, A. Maisonneuve, Paris 1952.

Filippani-Ronconi P., *Upaniṣad antiche e medie*, Boringhieri, Torino 1968.

Gambhirānanda Svāmi, *Eight Upaniṣads*, 2 vols., Advaita Āshrama, Calcutta 1956.

Hillebrandt A., *Aus Brahmaṇas und Upaniṣaden*, Düsseldorf und Köln 1964.

Hume R.E., *The Thirteen Principal Upanishads*, Oxford University Press, New York 1971.

Jha Ganganatha, *The Chāndogyopaniṣad*, Oriental Book Agency, Poona 1942.

Keith A.B., *Aitareya Āraṇyaka*, Oxford 1909, reprint 1969.

Lal P., *The Avyakta Upaniṣad*, Inter Culture, Thompson 1973.

Lal P., *The Īśa Upaniṣad*, Inter Culture, Thompson 1973.

Lal P., *The Mahānārāyaṇa Upaniṣad*, Inter Culture, Thompson 1973.

Lebail P., *Six Upanishads majeures (Kena, Muṇḍaka, Īsha, Kaṭha, Aitareya, Prashna)*, Le Courrier du Livre, Paris 1971.

Lesimple E., *Māṇḍūkya Upanishad*, 'Les Upanishad' vol. V, A. Maisonneuve, Paris 1944.

Lesimple E., *Taittirīya Upanishad*, 'Les Upanishad' vol. IX, A. Maisonneuve, Paris 1948.

Madhavānanda, *The Bṛhadāraṇyaka Upaniṣad with the commentary of Śaṁkarācārya*, Advaita Āshrama, Calcutta 1965.

Martin-Dubost P., *Muṇḍakopaniṣadbhāṣya*, Commentaire de Śaṁkara sur la *Muṇḍaka Upaniṣad*, Michel Allard Éditions Orientales, Paris 1978.

Maury J., *Muṇḍaka Upanishad*, 'Les Upanishad' vol. IV, A. Maisonneuve, Paris 1943.

Mitra R.L., *Chāndogya Upanishad*, 'Bibliotheca Indica', Calcutta 1862.

Müller M., *The Upanishads*, 'Sacred Books of the East', vols. I and XV, Motilal Banarsidass, reprint Delhi 1969.

Nikhilānanda Svāmi, *The Upanishads*, 4 vols., Phoenix House, London 1951–59.

Nikhilānanda Svāmi, *The Upanishads*, Allen and Unwin, London 1963.

Nikhilānanda Svāmi, *The Māṇḍūkyopanishad with Gauḍapāda's kārikā and Śaṁkara's commentary*, Śrī Rāmakrishna Āshrama, Mysore 1968.

Papesso V., *Chāndogya Upanishad*, Zanichelli, Bologna 1937.

Radhakrishnan S., *The Principal Upaniṣads*, Allen and Unwin, London 1974.

Raphael, *Cinque Upanishad (Īśa, Kaivalya, Brahmabindu, Sarvasāra, Atharvaśira)*, traduzione dal sanscrito e commento di Raphael, Edizioni Āśram Vidyā, Roma 1974.

Raphael, *Māṇḍūkya Upaniṣad con i versi-kārikā di Gauḍapāda e il commento di Śaṁkara*, traduzione dal sanscrito e note di Raphael, (con testo sanscrito). Roma 1976. Di Śaṁkara le Edizioni Āśram Vidyā hanno pubblicato, tradotte e commentate da Raphael, le opere: *Aparokṣānubhūti e Vivekacūḍāmaṇi*.

Raphael, *Māṇḍūkyakārikā* di Gauḍapāda, traduzione dal sanscrito e commento di Raphael (con testo sanscrito). Edizioni Āśram Vidyā, Roma 1981.

Renou L., *Īśa Upanishad*, 'Les Upanishad' Vol. I, A. Maisonneuve, Paris 1943.

Renou L., *Kaṭha Upanishad*, ibid, vol. II, 1943.

Renou L., *Kena Upanishad*, ibid, vol. III, 1943.

Renou L., *Kauṣītaki Upanishad*, ibid, vol. VI, 1948.

Renou L., *Bāṣkala-Mantra Upanishad*, ibid, vol. XVI, 1956.

Renou L., *Chāgaleya Upanishad*, ibid, vol. XVII, 1959.

Röer E., *Nine Upanishads (Taittirīya, Aitareya, Śvetāśvatara, Kena Īśa, Kauṣītaki, Praśna, Muṇḍaka, Māṇḍūkya)*, 'Bibliotheca Indica', Calcutta 1853.

Röer E., *The Brihad Āranyaka Upanishad*, Elysium Press, Calcutta 1908.

Senart E., *Bṛhadāraṇyaka-upaniṣad*, Collection Emile Senart, vol. III, Les Belles Lettres, Paris 1967.

Senart E., *Chāndogya-upanishad*, ibid., vol. I, Paris 1930.

Sharvānanda Svāmi, *Aitareyopaniṣad Īśavasyopaniṣad, Kaṭhopaniṣad, Kenopaniṣad, Muṇḍakopaniṣad, Praśnopaniṣad, Taittirīyopaniṣad*, Vedānta Press 1974.

Sheshacarri V.C., *The Īśa, Kena, Muṇḍaka Upanishads with Śaṁkarāchārya's commentary*, Madras 1905.
Sheshacarri V.C., *The Kaṭha and Praśna Upanishads, with Śaṁkarāchārya's commentary*, Madras 1923.
Sheshacarri V.C., *The Chāndogya Upanishad, with Śaṁkarāchārya's commentary*, Madras 1923.
Sheshacarri V.C., *The Aitareya and Taittirīya Upanishads, with Śaṁkarāchārya's commentary*, Madras 1923.
Siddhesvar Varma S., *Śvetāsvatara Upaniṣad*, Panini Office, Allahabad 1916.
Silburn A., *Śvetāśvatara Upanishad*, 'Les Upanishad', vol. VII, A. Maisonneuve, Paris 1948.
Silburn L., *Aitareya Upanishad*, ibid., vol. X, Paris 1950.
Śivānanda Svāmi, *Ten Upanishads*, Calcutta 1944.
Thieme P., *Upanishaden*, Stuttgart 1966.
Tubini B., *Atharvaśiras Upanishad*, 'Les Upanishad' vol. XI, A. Maisonneuve, Paris 1952.
Tubini B., *Brahmabindu Upanishad*, ibid, vol. XII, Paris 1952.
Tubini B., *Kaivalya Upanishad*, ibid, vol. XIII, Paris 1952.
Tubini B., *Sarvasāropanishad*, ibid, vol. XIV, Paris 1952.
Varenne J., *La Mahānārāyaṇa Upanishad et la Prāṇāgnihotra Upanishad*, 2 voll. De Boccard, Paris 1961.
Varenne J., *Gaṇapati Upanishad*, 'Les Upanishad' vol. XVIII, A. Maisonneuve, Paris 1965.
Varenne J., *Īśa Upanishad*, in 'Le Veda', Gerard et C., Verviers 1968.
Varenne J., *Upanishads du Yoga*, Paris 1971.
Varenne J., *Devī Upanishad*, 'Les Upanishad' vol. XIX, A. Maisonneuve, Paris 1971.
Vasu S.C., *The Upaniṣads (Īśa, Kena, Kaṭha, Praśna, Muṇḍaka and Māṇḍūkya)* repr. of 1909 ed. AMS Press, New York.
Vasu S.C., *Chāndogya Upaniṣad*, repr. of 1919 ed. AMS Press, New York.
Vasu S.C., *The Bṛhadāranyaka Upaniṣad*, repr. of 1916 ed. AMS Press, New York.

Wade A., *Ten Principal Upanishads*, Gordon Press, New York s.d.

Brahma-sūtra

Apte V.M., *Brahma-Sūtra-Shaṁkara-Bhāṣya*, Popular Book Depot, Bombay 1960.

Date V.H., *Vedānta Explained, Śaṁkara's commentary on the Brahma-sūtra*, 2 vols, Bookseller's Publishing Co., Bombay 1954.

Gambhirānanda Svāmi, *Brahma-Sūtra Bhāṣya of Śaṁkarācārya*, Advaita Āshrama, Calcutta 1972.

Karmarkar R.D., *Śrī-bhāṣya*, University of Poona, vols. 3, Poona 1959–64.

Radhakrishnan S., *The Brahma-Sūtra*, Allen and Unwin, London 1960 (reprint of 1960, Greenwood 1968).

Rau S.S., *Pūrṇaprajña-darśana (Vedānta-Sūtra with the commentary of Śrī Madhvācārya)* Madras s.d.

Renou L., *Prolégomènes au Vedānta*, Paris 1951.

Thibaut G., *The Vedānta Sūtras with the commentary of Śaṁkarācārya*, Sacred Books of the East, vols. XXXIV, XXXVIII, Motilal Banarsidass, Delhi reprint 1968.

Thibaut G., *The Vedānta Sūtras with the commentary of Rāmānujācārya*, Sacred Books of the East, vol. XLVIII, Motilal Banarsidass, Delhi reprint 1966.

Vecchiotti I., *Brahmasūtra*, testo sanscrito, con introduzione, traduzione, commento e lessico. Astrolabio-Ubaldini, Roma 1979.

Vedānta-Sūtras with the commentary of Śrī Madhvācārya, Śrī Vyāsa Press, Tirupati 1936.

Bhagavad-Gītā

Arnold E., *The Song Celestial or Bhagavad Gītā*, Routledge and Kegan Paul Ltd, London 1972.

Bhaktivedanta Svāmi Prabhupāda, *La Bhagavad Gītā com'è*,

Bhaktivedanta Book Trust (traduzione italiana) 1976.
Chidbhavānanda, *The Bhagavad Gītā*, Śrī Rāmakrishna Tapovanam Publication Section, 1974.
Cogni, G., *La Bhagavad Gītā*, (in versi), Ceschina, Milano 1973. Seconda edizione, Roma 1980.
Edgerton F., *The Bhagavad Gītā*, 2 vols. Harvard University Press, Cambridge 1952.
Esnoul A.M., *Bhagavad Gītā*, Adelphi, Milano 1976.
Garbe R., *Die Bhagavadgītā*, Leipzig 1905.
Gnoli, R., *Bhagavadgītā*, il testo tradotto è la recensione Kashmira con il commento di Abhinavagupta. Utet, Torino 1976.
Hill W.D.P., *The Bhagavadgītā*, Oxford University Press, Oxford 1928.
Kamensky A., *Bhagavadgītā*, Le Courrier du Livre, Paris 1964.
Kerbaker M., *Bhagavad-Gītā*, (in ottave) a cura di C. Formichi e V. Pisani, R. Accademia d'Italia, Roma 1936.
Kirby M.L. e Jinarajadasa, *La Bhagavad Gītā o Poema Divino*, Alaya, Milano 1935.
Nazari O., *Il Canto Divino*, Palermo 1904.
Nataraja Guru, *The Bhagavad Gītā*, Asia Publishing House, London 1961.
Pizzagalli A.M., *La Bhagavadgītā*, Carabba, Lanciano 1917.
Radhakrishnan S., *Bhagavad Gītā*, Astrolabio-Ubaldini. Roma 1964.
Raphael, *Bhagavad Gītā*, traduzione dal sanscrito e commento di Raphael, Edizioni Āśram Vidyā, Roma 1974. Seconda edizione ampliata e con il testo sanscrito translitterato, Roma 1982.
Rau S.S., *Bhagavad Gītā*, Natesan, Madras 1906.
Sastri M.A., *The Bhagavad-Gītā*, with the commentary of Śrī Śaṅkarācārya, Ramasvami Sastrulu and Sons, Madras 1972.
Telang K.T., *The Bhagavadgītā with the Sanatsujātiyā and the Anugītā*, Sacred Books of the East, vol. VIII, Motilal

Banarsidass, Delhi reprint 1970.
Vassalini I., *Bhagavadgītā*, (in esametri), Laterza, Bari 1943.
Zaehner R.C., *The Bhagavad Gītā with a Commentary based on the Original Sources*, Oxford University Press, Oxford 1969.

c) *Studies, essays and monographs concerning Vedānta:*

Abhedānanda Svāmī, *The Vedānta Philosophy, Self-Knowledge.* Vedānta Society, New York 1905.
Abhedānanda Svāmī, *Three Lectures on Vedānta Philosophy.* Calcutta 1935.
Abhedānanda Svāmī, *Unity and Armony.* Calcutta 1936.
Abhedānanda Svāmī, *The Path of Realization.* Calcutta 1939.
Abhedānanda Svāmī, *Attitude of Vedānta towards Religion.* Calcutta 1947.
Abhedānanda Svāmī, *An introduction to the philosophy of Pañcadaśī.* Calcutta 1948.
Aiyar B.R.R., *Rambles in the Vedānta.* Madras 1905.
Aiyar N.S., *Vedānta and the three Policies.* Madras 1914.
Aiyar R.K., *Outlines of Vedānta.* Bombay.
Aiyer K.S., *The Vedānta and its ethical aspect.* Śrīraṁgam 1923.
Albertson Edwards S., *Vedānta*, Sherbourne Press, Los Angeles 1970.
Anandacarya, *Brahmadarśanam or intuition of the Absolute.* London 1917.
Apte R.N., *The doctrine of māyā: its existence in the Vedantic sūtra, and development in later Vedānta*, Bombay 1896.
Ātmananda S. Svāmi, *Ātmajñāna made easy.* Amritsar 1937.
Ātmananda S. Svāmi, *Śaṁkara's teachings in his own words.* Bhavan Books Univ. Bombay 1960.
Ayyar K.A.K., *Vedānta or the science of reality.* Holenarsipur 1965.
Ballantyne J.R., *Christianity contrasted with Hindu philosophy.* Madras 1860.

Barnett L.D., *Brahma-Knowledge*: an outline of the philosophy of the Vedānta, as set forth by the Upanishads and by Śaṁkara. Murray, London 1907.
Belvarkar S.K., *Lectures on Vedānta*. Belvakujna Publ. House, Poona 1929.
Bhaktisiddhanta Gosvami, *Few words on Vedānta*. Madras 1957.
Bhashyacarya N., *The age of Śrī Śaṁkarācārya*. Theosophical Publ. House, Adyar-Madras 1915.
Bhattacarya A.S., *Studies in post-Śaṁkara dialectics*, University of Calcutta, Calcutta 1936.
Bhattacarya K.C., *Studies in Vedantism*. University of Calcutta, Calcutta 1909.
Bhattacarya K., *An introduction to Advaita Philosophy*, University of Calcutta, Calcutta 1924.
Bhattacarya V., *The Āgamaśāstra of Gauḍapāda*. University of Calcutta 1943.
Bhumananda Tirtha, *Vedantic way of living*. Paralam 1970.
Biardeau M., *La Philosophie de Maṇḍana Miśra vue a partir de la Brahmasiddhi*. Paris 1969.
Buch M., *The philosophy of Śaṁkara*. Baroda 1921.
Cakraborty N.B., *The Advaita concept of falsity, a Critical Study*, Calcutta 1967.
Cakravarti S.C., *Theory of Unreality*. Calcutta 1922.
Camman K., *Das System des Advaita nach der Lehre des Prakās 'ātman*, O. Harrassowitz, Wiesbaden 1965.
Chatterjee C., *Vedantic Education*. Lucknow 1957.
Chattopadhyay B.K., *Upanishad; the philosophy of Śaṁkara and Rāmānuja*. Calcutta 1971.
Chaudhuri R., *Sūfism and Vedānta*. Calcutta 1945–1948.
Chaudhuri A.K.R., *Self and falsity in Advaita Vedānta*. Progressive Publishers, Calcutta 1955.
Chethimattam J.B., *Consciousness and Reality: Indian approach to Metaphysics*. London 1971.
Cohen S.S., *Advaitic sādhanā*, Motilal Banarsidass, Delhi 1975.

Conio C., *Philosophy of Gauḍapāda's Māṇḍūkya kārikā*. Varanasi 1970.

Dandoy G., *L'ontologie du Vedānta*. Paris 1932.

Dandoy G.S.J., *Essay on the Doctrine of the Unreality of the world in the Advaita*. Calcutta 1919.

Das R., *Introduction to Shankara*, Firma K.L. Mukhopadhyay, Calcutta 1968.

Das R.V., *The Essential of Advaitism*, Motilal Banarsidass, Lahore 1933.

Das S.K., *Towards a Systematic Study of Vedānta*, University of Calcutta, Calcutta 1931.

Das S.K., *A study of the Vedānta*, University of Calcutta, Calcutta 1937.

Dasgupta S.N., *The logic of Vedānta*, London 1922.

Dasgupta S.N., *Indian Idealism*, Cambridge University Press, Cambridge 1962.

Date V.H., *Vedānta explained: Śaṁkara's Commentary on the Brahma-sūtra*, Verry 1974.

De Smet R., *The theological method of Śaṁkara*, (Dissertazione), Roma 1953.

Deussen P., *The System of the Vedānta*, Dover Pbns. 1973.

Deussen P., *Erinnerungen an Indien*, Kiel 1904.

Deutsch E., *Advaita Vedānta: A philosophical reconstruction*, University Press of Hawaii, Honolulu 1969.

Deutsch e Buitenen Van J.A., *Source Book of Advaita Vedānta*, University Press of Hawaii, Honolulu 1971.

Devanandan P.D., *The Concept of Māyā*, Imca Publ. House, Calcutta 1954.

Devaraja N.K., *An introduction to Śaṁkara's theory of Knowledge*, Motilal Barnarsidass, Delhi 1962.

Dutt N.K., *Vedānta: its place as a system of metaphisics*, Calcutta 1931.

Divivedi M.N., *Monism or Advaitism?*, Subhoda-Prakasa Press, Bombay 1889.

Ghate V.S., *The Vedānta*, Bhandarkar Oriental Research Institute, Poona 1960.

Griffith B., *Vedānta and Christian faith*, Dawn Horse Press 1973.
Grousset R., *Les philosophies indiennes. Les systèmes*, Biblioteque française, Paris 1931.
Guenon R., *Introduzione generale allo studio delle dottrine indù*, Edizioni Studi Tradizionali, Torino 1965.
Guenon R., *L'uomo e il suo divenire secondo il Vedānta*, Edizioni Studi Tradizionali, Torino 1964.
Guenon R., *Il simbolismo della croce*, Edizioni Studi Tradizionali, Torino 1964.
Guenon R., *Gli stati molteplici dell'Essere*, Edizioni Studi Tradizionali, Torino 1965.
Gupta G.P., *Vedānta for The West*, Lucknow 1927.
Gupta S., *Studies in the Philosophy of Madhusūdana Sarasvatī*, Calcutta 1966.
Hacker P., *Vivarta: Studien zur Geschichte der illusionisstichen Kosmologie und Erkenntnistheorie der Inder*, Akademie der Wissenschaft, Wiesbaden 1953.
Hacker P., *Untersuchungen über die texte des frühen Advaitavāda*, Die Schuler Śaṅkaras, Wiesbaden 1950.
Hacker P., *Die Idee der Person im Denken von Vedānta-Philosophen*, 'Studia Missionalia' vol. XIII, 1963.
Harrison M.H., *Hindu Monism and Pluralism*. London 1932.
Hasurkar S.S. *Vācaspati Miśra on Advaita Vedānta*, Mithila Institute, Darbhanga 1958.
Haughton G.C., *The exposition of the Vedānta Philosophy*. London 1835.
Heinrich W., *Verklärung und Erlösung in Vedānta*, Salzburg 1956.
Herbert J., *Vedantisme et vie pratique*, Paris 1942.
Hoang-Sy-Quy, *Le Moi qui me depasse selon le Vedānta*, Saigon 1971.
Husain J.A.M., *A Christian's view of Vedānta*, Tiruchirapalli.
Isherwood C., *Vedānta for the Western World*, Allen and Unwin, London 1963.

Isherwood C., *Vedānta for Modern Man*, Allen and Unwin, London 1952.

Isherwood C., *Approach to Vedānta*, Vedānta Press, Hollywood 1970.

Iyer K.A.K., *Vedānta, or the Science of Reality*, Ganesh and Co., Madras 1930.

Iyer V.M.K., *Advaita Vedānta according to Śaṁkara*, Asia Publ. House, Bombay 1964.

Jagannatha S., *Advaitāmṛta*, Poona 1965.

Jha Ganganatha, *Śaṁkara's Vedānta in Its Sources*, Allahabad 1939.

Jha R., *The Vedantic and the Buddhist concept of Reality as interpreted by Śaṁkara and Nagarjuna*, South Asia Bks 1973.

Johanns P., *Vers le Christ par le Vedānta*, Louvain 1932.

Johnson C. e Prabhavananda Svāmi, *Vedānta: An Anthology of Hindu scripture, commentary and poetry*, Vedānta Press, Bantam 1974.

Karapatrasvami, *Advaitabodhadīpikā (Lamp of non-dual knowledge)*. Tiruvannamalai 1960.

Karmarkar A.P., *Comparison of the Bhāshya of Śaṁkara, Rāmānuja, Keśavakāśmīrin and Vallabha on some Crucial Sūtras*, Poona 1920.

Kashinath, *The scientific Vedānta*, Intl. Pbns. Serv. 1974.

Keller C.A., *Die Vedāntaphilosophie und die Christusbotschaft*, Basel 1952.

Kirtikar V.J., *Studies in Vedānta*, Bombay 1924.

Krisnananda S. Svāmi, *The realisation of the Absolute according to the Upanishad*, Rishikes 1952.

Lacombe O., *L'Absolu selon le Vedānta*. Geuthner, Paris 1966.

Laksminarayana K., *Cultural socialism or Vedānta*. Tevali 1971.

Le Saux H., *Eveil à soi – Eveil à Dieu*. Alençon 1971.

Le Saux H., *Sagesse hindoue – Mistique chretienne. Du Vedānta a la Trinité*. Paris 1965.

Levy J., *Immediate knowledge and happiness: non-dualistic Vedānta*. Abingdon 1951.

Levy J., *The Nature of Man According to the Vedānta*. Routledge and Kegan, London 1956.
Mahadevan T.M.P., *The Philosophy of Advaita*. Vedānta Pr. London 1938.
Mahadevan T.M.P., *Gauḍapāda, a study in Early Advaita*, Univ. of Madras, Madras 1960.
Mahadevan T.M.P., *The study of Advaita*. London 1957.
Mahadevan T.M.P., *The sambandhavārttika of Sureśvarācārya*. Madras 1958.
Mahadevan T.M.P., *Preceptors of Advaita*. Secunderabad 1968.
Mahadevan T.M.P., *Insights of Advaita*. Mysore 1970.
Mahadevan T.M.P., *Śaṁkarācārya*, National Book Trust, New Delhi 1968.
Mainkar T.G., *A comparative study of the commentaries on the Bhagavad-Gītā*, Delhi 1969.
Majumdar S., *The Vedānta philosophy*. Published by S.N. Bhattacharya, Bankipore 1926.
Malhotra S.L., *Social and political orientation of Neo-Vedantism*, Verry 1970.
Malkani G.R., *Ajñāna* (a Symposium), London 1933.
Malkani G.R., *Philosophy of the Self*. Amalner 1939.
Malkani G.R., *Vedantic Epistemology*. The Indian Institute of Philosophy, Amalner 1953.
Malkani G.R., *Metaphysics of Advaita Vedānta*. Amalner 1961.
Martin-Dubost P., *Śaṁkara e il Vedānta*. Edizioni Āśram Vidyā, Roma 1989.
Metha S.S., *A Manual of Vedānta philosophy*. Bombay 1919.
Mishra A.P., *The development and place of Bhakti in Śaṁkara's Vedānta*. Allahabad 1969.
Mohatta Ramgopal, *Vedānta in practice*, Ed. Bharatiya Vidyā, Bombay 1970.
Morretta A., *Il pensiero Vedānta*. Abete, Roma 1968.
Mugdal S.G., *Advaita of Śaṁkara. A reappraisal*. Motilal Barnarsidass, Delhi 1975.
Mukerji A.C., *The nature of the Self*. Allahabad 1938.

Mukherji N., *A study of Śaṁkara*. University of Calcutta, Calcutta 1942.
Mukherji P., *Introduction to Vedānta philosophy*. Calcutta 1928.
Mukhopadyaya P.N., *The fundamentals of Vedānta philosophy*. Madras 1961.
Müller M.F., *Three lectures on the Vedānta philosophy*, London 1894.
Müller M.F., *The six systems of Indian philosophy*, reprint of 1919 Intl. Pbns. Serv., 1973.
Murty Satchidananda, *Revelation and Reason in Advaita Vedānta*. Columbia University Press, New York 1961.
Nakamura H., *Shoki Vedānta Tetsugaku shi*, Tokyo 1950–1956.
Nikam N.A., *Vedānta-delight of Being*, Mysore 1970.
Nikhilānanda Svāmi, *L'uomo alla ricerca dell'immortalità*, Edizioni Āśram Vidyā, Roma 1989.
Nityabodhānanda Svāmi, *Le chemin de la perfection selon le Yoga-Vedānta*, La Colombe, Paris 1960.
Otto R., *West-östliche Mystik, Vergleich und Unterscheidung zur Vesendeutung*, Gotha 1926.
Otto R. e Mohr J.C., *Dīpikā des Nivāsa*, Tübingen 1916.
Pande S.L., *The old Advaita Vedānta*. Ed. M.S. Sahitcharya, Calcutta.
Panikkar R., *Māyā e Apocalisse*, Abete, Roma 1966.
Papali C.B., *The Advaita Vedānta of Śaṁkarācārya*, Teresianum, Roma 1964.
Pessein J.F., *Vedānta vindicated or harmony of Vedānta and Christian philosophy*. Trichinopoly 1925.
Piantelli M., *Śaṁkara e la rinascita del Brāhmanesimo*, Esperienze, Fossano 1974.
Pratyagatmananda Svāmi, *Fundamentals of Vedānta philosophy*, Vedānta Press.
Radhakrishnan S., *The ethics of the Vedānta and its metaphysical presuppositions*. Madras 1908.
Radhakrishnan S., *The Vedānta according to Śaṁkara and Rāmānuja*. London 1928.
Radhakrishnan S., *The Philosophy of the Upanishads*, London 1924.

Raju P.T., *Idealistic thought of India*, reprint of 1953, Johnson Repr., London 1973.

Ramakrishnraw K.B., *Ontology of Advaita with special reference to māyā*. Mulki 1964.

Ramananda Tirtha, *A writer's study of Śaṁkara versus the six Preceptors of Advaita*. Madras 1970.

Ranade R.D., *Vedānta; the culmination of Indian thought*. Bombay 1970.

Ranade R.D., *A constructive survey of Upanishadic philosphy*. Oriental Book Agency, Poona 1926.

Rao K.B., *Three lectures on Advaita as philosophy and religion*. Mysore 1969.

Rao P.N., *Introduction to Vedānta*. Bhavan's Book Univ. Bombay 1960.

Rao P.N., *The philosophy of A.N. Whitehead in the light of the Advaita Vedānta of Śaṁkara*. Tirupati 1966.

Rao S.K., *Śaṁkara: a psychological study*. Mysore 1960.

Rao P.N., *The schools of Vedānta*. Bombay 1943.

Reyna R., *The concept of Māyā*. Bombay 1962.

Saccidanandendrasarasvati, *The Great Equation; an exposition of the doctrine of Advaita Vedānta*. Bombay 1963.

Saccidanandendrasarasvati, *How to recognize the Method of Vedānta*. Holenarsipur 1964.

Saccidanandendrasarasvati, *Śaṁkara's clarification of certain Vedantic concepts*. Holenarsipur 1964.

Saccidanandendrasarasvati, *Salient Features of Śaṁkara's vedānta*, Holenarsipur 1967.

Sankaranarayanan P., *What is Advaita?* Bhavan's Books Publ. Bombay 1971.

Santinatha Sadhu, *Māyāvāda, or the non-dualistic philosphy*. Poona 1938.

Sarda H.B., *Śaṁkara and Dayānand*. Ajmer 1944.

Sarma Y.S., *Avasthātraya, or the unique method of Vedānta*. Bangalore 1937.

Sastri P.D., *The doctrine of Māyā in the Philosophy of the Vedānta*. Luzac and Co. London 1911.

Satprakashananda Svāmi, *Method of knowledge according to Advaita Vedānta*. London 1965.
Sen B.N., *Philosophy of the Vedānta*. Calcutta 1903.
Sengupta B.K., *A Critique of the Vivaraṇa School* (Studies in some fundamental Advaitist theories). S.N. Sengupta, Murkhopadhya-Calcutta 1959.
Sharma C., *Dialectic in Buddhism and Vedānta*. Benares 1952.
Sharma R.N., *Reign of realism in Indian philosophy*. Madras 1937.
Sharma S.N., *The Teaching of Sarvajñātmā Muni*. Utrecht 1954.
Shastri K., *An introduction to Advaita Philosophy*, Univ. of Calcutta, Calcutta 1926.
Shastri K., *A realistic interpretation of Śaṁkara's Vedānta*. Calcutta 1931.
Shrivastava S.N.L., *Śaṁkara and Bradley*. Delhi 1968.
Siddheśvarānanda Svāmi, *Essai sur la Métaphysique du Vedānta*. Angers 1948.
Siddheśvarānanda Svāmi, *Quelques aspects de la philosophie vedantique*. Paris 1941–42.
Siddheśvarānanda Svāmi, *La meditation selon le yoga Vedānta*, A. Maisonneuve, Paris 1955.
Siddheśvarānanda Svāmi, *L'intuition metaphysique*. Paris 1959.
Siddheśvarānanda Svāmi, *Pensiero indiano e Mistica carmelitana*, Edizioni Āśram Vidyā, Roma 1977.
Singh R.P., *The Vedānta of Śaṁkara, a Metaphysics of Value*, vol. I, Bharat Publishing House, Jaipur 1949.
Singh Satyavrata, *Vedantade śika*. Varanasi 1958.
Sinha D., *The idealist standpoint, a study in the vedantic metaphysics of experience*. Santiniketan 1965.
Sircar M., *Comparative studies in Vedāntism*. Humphrey University of Calcutta, Calcutta 1927.
Sircar M., *The system of Vedantic thought and culture*. University of Calcutta 1927.
Śivānanda Svāmi, *Vedānta and Freedom*. Rishikes 1937.
Śivānanda Svāmi, *Vedānta in daily life*. Amritsar 1937.
Śivānanda Svāmi, *First Lessons in Vedānta*. Rishikes 1952.

Śivānanda Svāmi, *Vedānta for beginners*. Rishikes 1960.
Sprung G.M., *The problems of two truths in Buddhism and Vedānta*. Reidel Pub. 1973.
Srinivasa C.T., *The rational basis of the Mahāvākyas*. Madras 1930.
Srinivasachari D.N., *Śaṁkara and Rāmānuja*. Madras 1913.
Srinivasachari P.N., *A synthetic view of Vedānta*. The Adyar Library. Madras 1954.
Srinivasachari P.N., *Advaita and Viśiṣṭādvaita*. Bombay 1961.
Srinivasam G., *The existentialist concept of the hindu philosophical systems*. Allahabad 1967.
Staal J.F., *Advaita and Neo Platonism; a critical study in comparative philosophy*, Univ. of Madras, Madras 1961.
Sundaram P.K., *Advaita epistemology*. Madras 1970.
Tattvabhusham S., *The Vedānta and its relation to modern thought*. Calcutta 1901.
Tripathi M.S., *A sketch of the Vedānta philosophy*. Bombay 1901.
Upadhyaya V.P., *Lights on Vedānta*, 'Chowkhamba Sanskrit Series', vol. VI, Varanasi 1959.
Urquhart W.S., *The Vedānta and Modern Thought*. Oxford Univ. Press. London 1928.
Varma P.M., *Role of Vedānta as a universal religion and science of self-realisation*. Allahabad 1959–1960.
Venkataraman S., *Selected works of Śrī Śaṁkara*. (Text and translation) Madras.
Vidyatatna Sastri K., *An Introduction to Advaita Philosophy*. Calcutta 1924.
Vivekānanda Svāmi, *Jñāna yoga*, Astrolabio-Ubaldini, Roma 1963.
Von Glasenapp H., *Der stufenweg zum Gottliche Śaṁkara's Philosophie der All-Einheit*. Baden-Baden 1948.
Von Glasenapp H., *Vedānta und Buddhismus*. Wiesbaden 1950.
Warrier A.G., *The concept of Mukti in Advaita Vedānta*. Madras 1961.
Walleser M., *Der ältere Vedānta*, Geschichte, Kritik und Lehre Heidelberg 1910.

Windischmann F.H., *Śaṁkara*. Bonn 1831.
Windischmann F.H., *Śaṁkara sive de theologumenis Vedanticorum*. Bonn 1833.
Wood E.E., *La filosofia del Vedānta, (The glorious presence)*, Astrolabio-Ubaldini, Roma 1976.
Woodley E.C., *A brief exposition of the Saṁkhya and Vedānta systems of Indian philosophy*. Calcutta 1907.
Woods J.H. e Runkle C.B., *Outline of the Vedānta system of philosophy according to Śaṁkara*. London 1917.